# Discovering the Essence

## How to Grow a Spiritual Practice When Your Religion Is Cracking Apart

# Discovering the Essence

## How to Grow a Spiritual Practice When Your Religion Is Cracking Apart

🌿🌿🌿🌿🌿🌿🌿🌿🌿🌿🌿🌿🌿🌿

### JEFF CAMPBELL

ANAMCHARA BOOKS

**ANAMCHARA BOOKS**

Vestal, New York 13850

www.AnamcharaBooks.com

Paperback ISBN: 978-1-62524-780-3
Ebook ISBN: 978-1-62524-781-0

Cover design by Ellyn Sanna.
Interior layout by Micaela Grace.
Cover photograph by Weerapat Kiatdumrong.
Hands with leaf icon by Ponsuwan (Dreamstime.com).
Leaf border illustration by Cat Vec (Dreamstime.com).

# Contents

My journey to the essence
was only possible because of
the love and support of so
many beautiful people.

This book is dedicated to them:
Mom and Dad, Bonnie,
Kiley, Storey, Gwyneth
and Ethan, Billy, Colleen,
Geoff, Jason, Marty, Lucas,
Lyanna, Zach, and Christine.

# Introduction

You are going to be okay.

There will come a time that this "new normal" will simply become normal. There will be ways in which your future life will be much, much better than it was. There are ways in which it will be worse. Mostly, it will simply be different.

You are going to be okay.

It's not fun to be in that no-man's land between *this* and *that*. It is scary and lonely. But you are going to be okay.

There are many different names for a spiritual transition. Each of them carries certain assumptions about the experience. None of these terms are perfect. But they all point to the exact opposite of the situation described in those timeless words of "Amazing Grace": not "I once was lost but now am found," but rather *we once were found but now are lost.* Perhaps we also feel as though we now are blind, when we once could see.

We might call this *liminal* space. Now we are *between* two states of being. Broadly, literally speaking, liminal space can be as simple as the walk between the living room and the bedroom. Or as heart-rending as the first night in an empty bed. It is that time when we live without a script. This book is most directly aimed at the millions occupying liminal space as we transition out of the faith communities that served us for a season of our lives.

This spiritual transition has also been described as a descent into our personal underworld. We are like some mythological figure, traveling within ourselves, to face the ghosts of our past. In his life-changing book *Falling Upward,* Richard Rohr describes this as spirituality for the second half of our life. According to this metaphor, we began by building a symbolic castle. Then we find ourselves leaving the castle that once seemed so precious to us.

A term for this sort of transition is *deconstruction.* Typically, *deconstruction* refers to the process of realizing a fundamentalist religious tradition (often evangelical Christianity) taught us many things that simply were not true. The act of deconstructing is the act of reclaiming and disentangling the truth from the falsehood, and, more important, coming to know and to name the actual purpose of the things that were believed.

This is one of my favorite terms to describe this time—and yet at the same time, it is also one of my least-favorite words to describe this time. Deconstruction was appropriated from postmodern philosophy. This group of staunch atheists would probably be rather upset at what has been applied to their terminology, since the term refers to a theory of literary criticism that questions traditional assumptions about certainty, identity, and truth. It was not originally intended to apply to a person's religious beliefs.

Nonetheless, it is a term that works for a spiritual experience in a wide variety of ways. One of the elements of the word's original meaning that has been maintained is the focus on discovering what the real purpose of our beliefs are. For example, we might once have thought that we believe in an angry God because God is in fact angry. Through an act of deconstruction, we might come to see that this view says more about our relationship with our own physical and earthly father than it has to do with the actual Creator of the universe.

The thing that all these different terms have in common, however, is that they denote the work of a person who is struggling to discover the essence of spirituality. A journey through liminal space is one that hopes to find a meaningful destination. A descent into the underworld is terrifying, but surely there must be something precious we are after if we are willing to undertake it. Rohr's spirituality for the second half of life is one characterized by a search for a deeper meaning than we knew before. Deconstruction is an act of finding what is nonnegotiable and of prime importance. Discovering the essence is one of the most important things we will ever do.

At the time I began my season of transition, I thought maybe it was the worst thing that had ever happened to me. As I look back on it, I think just maybe it was one of the best. I wish somebody had told me that someday I would see the whole thing in such a different light. That is why I am writing this book: out of my desire that I might be that person for you.

So I'll say it again: it is going to be okay. It is going to be more than okay. It might just be the best thing that has ever happened to you.

Permit me a little bit of autobiography here. Once, I was the token liberal at a fairly moderate Evangelical American church. I was happy in my role there. I was loved, and I loved others. I learned some important things there, not the least of which was how to begin to follow Jesus.

That was good. Until it wasn't good.

Some difficult events in my life did more than challenge the worldview I had taken on in that church: they challenged a number of fundamental things I had always believed about the world itself. Suddenly, philosophical questions were no longer abstractions. I experienced firsthand the idea that really bad things can happen to people who don't deserve them.

To be honest, I was disappointed in the people in that community I loved. Looking back, I can say that they did their best. And I can hardly blame them. I wasn't equipped for the things that were going on. How can I expect them to have been equipped to support me when I was hardly equipped to handle the situation myself?

I began to experience debilitating depression and anxiety. I was desperate for some new solution, since the old ones were not working. I widened my horizons, explored voices and thinkers outside the recommended reading list my church community prescribed. I began to hear murmurings from some of the wise folks who were just beginning to make it onto my spiritual radar. These people—whom I would not have taken seriously before—were saying a few of the same things, over and over.

I heard them talk about contemplation, meditation, and other spiritual practices.

It was hard to determine just what all that meant. As my old support system crumbled, I tried to figure out what these new things were. I mean, I had heard of them. Even flirted with them in the days before I was a Christian. But I didn't really know how to do them. I didn't know how or why they might be the answer to some of my problems, especially my dwindling financial and emotional resources. Though these thinkers, writers, and podcasters were quite clear that you should do these spiritual practices, there weren't many who were sharing specific details about how you do them.

And of the people who were willing to explain, many were trying to share this information in a way that would have cost more money than I had. Others seemed to be so territorial; there was only one way to do this, they implied. I had just come out of a tradition where that was the mantra: *There is only one way to do this*. I wasn't interested in trading one form of fundamentalism for another.

As I overcame those hurdles, however, I felt myself getting better. I discovered, firsthand, that I was safe and I was going to be okay. When

I was ready, I kept a promise to myself that I had made some time before. I did what I could, in my own small way, to try to make things easier for the people who walked a trail similar to mine.

This began with small contemplative groups at the progressive church I attended by that time. I eventually began facilitating day-long contemplative retreats. From there, I put together a website, *The Faithing Project,* and engaged in e-mail and social media-based explorations of different spiritual exercises. Most recently, I have widened my reach again with ebooks and paperbacks, presenting ways to build and deepen spiritual practices.

One of the key differences between the person I am today and the person I was a few years ago is that I am much less interested in the final outcome. I do not want to get you to come to our Sunday morning worship "experience" and then join my small group. I am not pitching a specific concept of heaven (and how to get there). I always struggled with the idea that a person needed to say one specific prayer so that they could be "saved" (whatever that meant). I am now convinced that's foolishness. I am much more interested in the process; the journey, not the destination.

Going through a spiritual transition—deconstructing—*is* a process. I do not have an agenda or desire that this process lead you to one specific place. Maybe it will be a circular journey for you. Maybe you will return to the place you came from. Maybe you will end up an atheist. Maybe you will end up identifying yourself as a mystic, like me. Maybe you will convert to some other faith tradition.

No. Wait. Stop. Let me try some parts of that last paragraph again. . . . The truth is that I am doing my best to not have an agenda or desire that this process leads you to one specific place. Is there a part of me that has some ego-centered hopes that you will come through this book and end up sounding a lot like me?

Well, yes. There is. But I am working on keeping my ego in check. This is much easier to do when I own, name, and admit where it pops up its ugly head. But even while owning and admitting that this ego is a reality, I can also say that much of me truly does not have an agenda for you.

This is why the autobiography I furnished is rather abbreviated. The specifics of my case are not particularly important, because my desire for you is not that you end up precisely like me. Regardless of where this transition takes you, there are things we will have in common—and there are things I found useful that I'm pretty sure will be useful to you too.

Spiritual practices are very good for pretty much everybody, regardless of where that person is. But they can be a game changer in times of transition and deconstruction.

Still, because we are all headed to different destinations, because we are in varying places in our journey, there will be some things here that make sense to you. There will be others that do not. There will be some practices that come easily. There will be others that are difficult. To the extent that I can, I will use language and exercises that have broad levels of appeal.

I hope that you will hold a gentle love for yourself through this process. At the same time, I hope that you will push yourself—but only a little bit. Think about what it takes to get physically fit. If I consider doing a physical exercise, pushing myself a little bit is a good thing. A minor-level burn in my muscles, I know, is the feeling of the muscle building itself up. A mildly unpleasant tug in my hamstrings, as I slip into the yoga pose, is the feeling of the tendons stretching. With these physical exercises, I reach a point when I know it is time to stop. I know that it is no longer a healthy kind of hurt I am carrying in my body. And I know that sometimes, my body is so weak and vulnerable (like when I am recovering from the flu) that no exercise at all makes sense. There is a psychological, spiritual parallel here. Pushing myself a little bit, emotionally, is necessary for growth in the "muscle" of my soul. It will build itself back up stronger than before when appropriately challenged. But pushing myself too hard and too fast is not productive. There are times that my soul is so vulnerable (call it a spiritual sickness) that pushing myself at all is simply a bad plan. So please keep this in mind as you read and apply my advice for this voyage of discovery.

Each of the chapters that follow will begin with some observations about aspects of the journey, followed by two or more spiritual practices. Throughout this book, the descriptions of the practices will be set in a box, so that they are easy to find as you flip through. It might work to read the pages in a chapter in one sitting, and then to do the spiritual practices—and then be done with this work for the day. These chapters have a vaguely chronological flow, but in some ways, the various aspects all come at once.

Make no mistake: some of this work is wonderful and liberating—but some of it is tough. And it is all work. Some days, you will feel up to the work. It will be fun to learn new things and try new practices. Other days, it will be laborious to even physically turn the pages. You will feel angry at your community, angry at yourself, and possibly angry at me on these days. Perhaps you will read only a few pages on these days when it is hard. Perhaps you won't read anything at all. Whichever it is, you are going to be okay.

So what is the essence? People smarter than me have observed that religion is the place where God and humans meet. This implies an important question: just how much is God, and how much is human effort? This is no easy thing to answer. As we try to work out what is God-made and what is human-made, we begin to enter into a realm beyond words. Discovering the essence is a process, not a destination. The route we take to get there is as important as the place where we land. For all these reasons, I can't give you a clear-cut definition. You'll have to provide that for yourself, as you make this journey. But what I can do is tell you that if it's time for you to be moving on, it will, in so many ways, feel better once you begin.

My experience with spiritual practice has led me to identify myself as a Christ-centered mystic. I use the term carefully. By "mystic," I mean a person who believes that the boundaries we usually assume to be quite rigid are actually quite permeable. One of the boundaries we mystics are most interested in is the one between human and God. We generally believe that some measure of unity with God can be experienced. For me, this is the *essence* of my spiritual practice, the point of the whole thing.

Some people who engage in spiritual practice aren't mystics, however. They engage in these practices for quite different reasons. Most of the spiritual practices in this book will be useful for someone who is not a mystic. On the other hand, while a person could be a mystic and endorse on a theoretical level only the idea of Divine union, it's hard to understand why somebody would forego the actual experience. Therefore, most mystics have some sort of spiritual practice that goes along with a set of beliefs about how our oneness with God is experienced or enhanced.

I have a lovely sense of coming full circle as I sit down to write to people who are on the same journey I have been. You all are my people. It is nice to be here with you.

—Jeff Campbell

# CHAPTER ONE

❧❧❧❧❧❧❧❧❧❧❧❧❧❧❧❧❧❧❧

# Why Spiritual Practices?

There are lots of smart things to do when undergoing a spiritual transition. So why focus on contemplative activities?

Well, first off, many people were never before encouraged to pursue this path. Can you and I share a tin-foil-hat moment this early in the book? Can I tell you something that sounds like a conspiracy theory? I don't think it's an accident that many of us were steered clear of spiritual practice while involved in organized religion. Because the thing is, a mystic is hard to control. Institutional religion fears losing the ability to steer its people. There isn't much vested interest in teaching you practices that could decrease your dependence on organized religion's programs, teaching, and buildings.

In short, regardless of the *why*, the first reason to learn spiritual practices during spiritual transition is because most of us did not learn them before.

Second, this is a step you can begin now. You don't need to find a new community to begin meditating. Finding a new spiritual home might take a while. In the meantime, taking up these practices can be a powerful way to fill up some of the emptiness. Let's sit with this reality for a moment. Saying good-bye isn't easy. Sometimes we miss even the parts we know were never good for us. Spiritual practices can help us get through this difficult time.

Finally, spiritual practices can come bearing unique gifts. They can help build resources we might well need through the conflict and sadness that are likely to come out at this time. And they can increase our wisdom, insight, intuition, and discernment as we choose what is next for us.

Can we try our first practice now? It will be pretty straightforward. As you mentally prepare for this first practice, let's begin with a question:

How long would it be comfortable for you to just sit and breathe? I am not asking this rhetorically. It's just you, here, now. You can come up with a real answer. How long could you comfortably sit?

Would you try something for me? Add about 20 percent onto this time. When you are ready, just do it. Sit. There are a few things that some people do during this time of sitting. You can play around with focusing on your breath, if you like. Try to release your thoughts, if you want.

In the next paragraph after the practice description, I am going to explain why this practice is such a valuable thing. If you aren't ready to trust me yet, and want to know *why*, now, I get that. Maybe you ought to read that section before you begin and then sit for whatever length of time you have decided on.

## Practice I
## Just Sitting

- *If you have decided on a time, enter it into a timer.*

- *Just sit. Try to sit for the length of time you planned on.*

- *Pay attention to your breath, if that seems like a good thing to do.*

- *When you are done, congratulate yourself. It is not easy to sit and do nothing. But it is good. And important.*

## Noise, Busyness, and Clutter

We spend so much of our energy creating busyness and noise. And then we wallow in this chaos. On the surface, filling our individual moments with sounds and our overarching schedule with activities might not appear to be connected. But when we look beneath the surface, we see that both create a kind of clutter. Busyness clutters up our schedule. Noises clutter up the airspace around us with sounds we do not need.

The creation of this clutter is a way to shield and protect ourselves from our fears about the past and the future. Perseverating about what happened before or what is going to happen next is the root of anxiety for a lot of us. These fears are quite a bit like a hopelessly annoying dog I once knew. The dog lived with his family near a major street, and he would bark endlessly at the cars that drove by. To judge by his demeanor, he thought himself an apex predator. For the record? He would have to hop to reach my kneecaps. Again and again, however, he ran up to the limits of the fence as the cars passed by, as if he wished to charge at the vehicles.

If that dog could understand words, I would have asked him, "What's the big plan here? What, precisely, are you planning to do with that car if you did catch it?" Though I can only make a guess (as the dog did not speak English and I did not speak Yippy Dog), it seems like the end game was for him to sink his teeth around the car bumpers. (An impossibility, due to the relative sizes of the dog's jaw and the bumper.) But even supposing he could perform such a feat, this still leaves the question, "What now, dog?"

When we live these noisy, busy lives we are like the driver of a big truck who speeds up out of fear of this tiny but loud little creature. The simple reality? The truck is safe, and so are we. There is not a single thing the past or the future can do to hurt us. The truth is, though, that we could talk to the truck driver until we are blue in the face. But until he pulled up in front of the house and we let the little dog do his canine best to hurt the truck, the man might not truly believe that he is invulnerable.

# The Power of Sitting

We are like the truck driver. We can be told a hundred times that there is nothing our worries about the future or the past can do to us. Only when we give them the opportunity to do their worst, do we discover their worst is not very much.

This sitting and waiting is the very root of so many spiritual practices. Perhaps it is the root of all of them. There will be bells, whistles, and adornments. Changes in focus and alterations to the process. Some of these changes will give practitioners some tools to release their worries and fears. Some of them will bring about nice feelings of peace. In others, we will have to release our negative thoughts over and over and over again. Perhaps at these times, when we are repeatedly dismissing the thoughts, it will be tempting to think that we are doing it wrong, that we failed.

But here is the thing: every single session, we are still alive at the end of our time. For whatever duration we sat, we found that we could do it. We survived and made it through. Every single time, we learned that our fears and worries cannot hurt us. Every time, that yippy dog barked and barked. There was not a single time he carried the big truck away.

This chapter will conclude with a second practice. This is similar to the first. However, It will ask you to choose a body part to focus on through the breathing. There's a lot worth saying about reclaiming the body.

Focusing on bodily sensation has been made famous through the mindfulness movement. The strength in this practice seems to be rooted in the idea that our senses of touch, taste, smell, and sight do not have a memory. When we are putting our mental energy into our sense perceptions we are not focused on the future or the past.

In terms of sitting and breathing, many people find that the inside edge of the nostril (where the air comes in) is a useful point of focus. Others like to notice the feeling and warmth of the air as it leaves the body over the lips. Another popular place is the abdomen, perhaps with a hand there to feel the movement of the belly as the air comes in and out. Personally? I like to put my attention on my very lowest ribs, right at the spot where the elbows might rest if my arms were at my sides. Feeling the subtle movement as the air comes in and out is a powerful experience of being in the moment for me.

You might want to try each of these parts of the body. It is best to choose them one at a time, though. Trying to focus on more than one part of the body tends to lead to frustration.

If you are using a timer, ask yourself about how long you sat last time. How did that go for you? Will you sit for longer today? Go for shorter? Try this practice without a timer at all?

## Practice 2
## Being Aware of the Body

- *If you are using a timer, set it now.*

- *Place your feet flat on the floor.*

- *Inhale deeply through the nose and out through the mouth.*

- *Breathe deeply in and out a second time.*

- *Breathe deeply in and out a third time.*

- *With the next inhalation, choose a place on your body. Turn your attention to this area and be aware of how it feels with the deep breaths.*

- *Continue. As thoughts arise, be gentle with yourself and return your attention to your body.*

# CHAPTER TWO

## What Do I Believe Now?

One of the first things that most of us experience in times of spiritual transition is sudden questions within ourselves about what we believe. Perhaps those questions prompted the transition. Or maybe our loss of community comes first, and we suddenly discover that the things we said and we thought we believed weren't really ours at all. Maybe we just held on to them because we were worried about the cost of not believing them. When I was in a place where my membership depended on the things I believed, I didn't let myself know when I was doubting. We are not always very good at knowing when it is primarily about the community and when it is primarily about the belief system. Most of the time, these are all mixed together.

## Negative vs. Positive

A problem in unhealthy or immature communities is that while they might be very good at naming the things they are against, they don't tend to be as passionate about naming the things they are for. The list of beliefs they espouse is primarily negative. "X is wrong." "We don't believe in Y" In these stunted communities, knowing that we don't believe in this or that seems more important than knowing what we do believe.

When this has been our mindset, it can be hard to get out of it. It's always easier to criticize than it is to endorse something. If this negative outlook has defined us, we can find ourselves saying, "I don't believe in this anymore. Or that. Or the other thing," even after we have left the community behind. But we discover that we are out of practice in naming the things that we do believe in.

Surely we have to stand against some things. But standing against is easy. And not particularly helpful in many ways.

It can feel new and uncomfortable to shift from "What don't I believe?" to "What do I believe?" It can feel like a mad scramble. We must find something to hold on to. It is difficult to stand for something, to believe in it.

May I be the first to invite you to celebrate your newfound freedom? It can be hard to be excited for ourselves at these times. I do not want to bypass your suffering. I know that it can be so very difficult. And yet, this is a wonderful time. You get to determine who you will be. I hope that you will honor this time and process. There's no need to not rush into whatever your next steps will be. Try on some beliefs. Consider whether they fit. Check in with the people who are proponents of them. See how it works for them. Sit with these new aspects of your identity.

Many people resist spiritual transitions because they fear powerlessness in the process, as though the transformation is an express train that we can't exit until the end of the line. But this is not how I, and many others, experienced the process.

What I see now is that I didn't experience much control or autonomy when I submitted my beliefs to a spiritual community that was not right for me. I was comparatively powerless where I was. Now? I am in control of every step.

The metaphorical train gives many opportunities to get off. You and I get to choose the things we believe. We will probably do this imperfectly. It can be tempting to perseverate on this last point: what if I choose wrong?

Probably we will choose poorly some of the time. But that does not mean that we should stop trying. The reason that many of us outgrew our spiritual communities was precisely because they were unwilling to view spirituality as a growth process. They provide an end point and don't ever want us to leave—indeed, theirs is an express train with only one destination. You and I have chosen to remove ourselves from that train.

Understanding spiritual belief as a process, not a product, is fundamental to this book. Not only will this topic receive an entire chapter later on; the idea will also be intertwined with many of the other subjects that will arise.

An important part of the process is coming to terms with both the positives and the negatives of where we are coming from. It can be easy to romanticize those former spiritual homes—almost as easy as it is to demonize them. But let's agree to be on our guard. We can't operate as though that old community gets to be considered "right" and lay on every alternative a burden of proof it can never live up to. We also won't get very far if we simply assume where we were was wrong in every possible way.

Which brings us back to the question: how do we decide what we believe now? We might not have ever truly done this for ourselves. We may have chosen a religion knowing that it would make all these decisions for us. Perhaps relying on other people's points of view was where we needed to be at that time. Toeing the party line was easy, fast, and convenient. Honest people will tell you that they sometimes miss some of the things about participating in a religion where someone else does all the heavy lifting. But you may have outgrown that mindset now. I know I did.

## Breath Prayers 101

As you move forward, slowly, into whatever is next for you, it is in your best interest to define yourself by who you are, rather than what you are against. It is wise to do this slowly, carefully, and with a gentle sense of humor.

For the spiritual practice we are going to try today, we are going to find a single sentence to endorse. Perhaps it feels like you have nothing now. It might seem like there is not a single thing that you believe in. If that describes you, start with love! In life in general, it is always good to start with love.

Consider the following phrases:

*God is love.*

*I am love.*

*I believe in love.*

*God is truth.*

*I believe in God.*

*I follow Jesus.*

*I believe in God.*

*I believe in Jesus.*

*Love is the answer.*

If none of those feel right, you can settle on a simple word—"love" or "peace"—or a favorite name for God, such as "Yahweh" or "Allah" or "Jesus."

The sentence or word you choose might be one in which you are quite comfortable. It might, on the other hand, be one with which you are struggling but want to believe. It might be one of those single words that just expresses your hope in that concept. If there is a phrase that is close to your heart but not on this list, then go with that.

Be sure it's short, about five words with not much more than two to three syllables per word. You should be able to say the phrase with a single inhalation.

You can also use visualizations with each inhale, with or without words. I will discuss visualizations more in a future chapter.

I have two images in particular that I like to use with the breath. One is to inhale and to see the breath as love and peace. Imagine the breath—and peace—coming into the lungs and spreading out into the whole of the body. Alternatively, I might breathe into parts of my body. I envision the breath going directly there. Of course we know that's not how breath works. But this knowledge doesn't seem to matter. I find it soothing and relaxing to breathe into areas, particularly if they are tense and hurting. I can then exhale the pain and hurt from each area. Throughout a session, I might keep all my focus on a headache, and repeatedly breathe into the same area. Or I can breathe into my entire body, starting with my feet and working my way up, for example.

One of the difficulties with contemplative practices is that there are a lot of different ways that people use the same term. The sort of practice we are going to try today is one I call a *breath prayer*. Some might have other names for this sort of practice, and others might not be thinking of exactly this kind of practice when they use the term "breath prayer."

A breath prayer (as I am using the term) is a contemplative activity that uses a part of the breath in an intentional way to explore or reinforce the meaning of a phrase or visualization. Before we get to that, let's explore a little more deeply the concept of how and when you might engage your practices in general.

It is good to commit to a certain length of time each day. In a lot of ways, sticking to the length you have decided on is more important than doing the practice for a long time. Using some sort of timer is a smart way to keep your time commitment. There are several apps for phones that are designed specifically for meditation. *Insight Meditation Timer* is one of my personal favorites.

The alternative to choosing a length of time is to do the practice for as long as it feels comfortable. The problem with this is that some of the best opportunities for growth, some of the real changes that contemplation brings about, occur only when we are uncomfortable. If we sit until we are suddenly anxious, frustrated, or focused on something else, we rob ourselves of the opportunity to work through these challenges. We deny ourselves the experience of knowing that we can make it through thinking and worrying about whatever it was that was starting to come up for us.

Let's return to the metaphor of the annoying dog. Imagine that the yard belonging to the dog is enormous. If the truck driver's plan is to drive past the house for only as long as is comfortable, he may never work up the nerve to completely pass the house. Each time, he might get part way there, then decide he is done, pull a U-turn, and return in the same direction he came from. In doing so he is forestalling his growth.

This is why I encouraged you to commit to a time in the last exercises, and it is why I will continue to do so. As we move into this next spiritual practice, how long are you going to plan to do it? The extremes here are, on the one hand, choosing such an extraordinarily long time that meditation comes to seem so difficult that you give up—and, at the other extreme, is choosing such a short time that you don't have the opportunity for growth, for change, for facing down that yippy dog.

For the sake of the exercise description, I am using the phrase "God is love." When you give this practice a try, use the phrase you have chosen.

# Practice 3
# A Breath Prayer

- *Place your feet flat on the floor. Sit up as straight as you comfortably can.*

- *Inhale.*

- *Exhale.*

- *Inhale.*

- *Exhale.*

- *Inhale. Think or say the sentence (and/or visualization) you chose (e.g., "God is love").*

- *Exhale.*

- *Inhale. Say or think your sentence again. Devote most of the time you have planned for this practice to this simple repetition. With each inhalation, say or think your sentence.*

- *When you are ready, release the words. Sit in a time of wordlessness. If thoughts intrude, come back gently to your word or phrase and repeat the process.*

The breath is of fundamental importance in spiritual practices. Introducing a phrase or sentence with the inhalation is a way of bringing the words into the body at the same time as the breath. There is another way: using specific words as you expel the breath. This carries a very different feel. We are sending those words out of us into the world with the air itself. These words might be a wish or hope for the world, something we want to purge from our own bodies, or something else that we are sending outside of us that comes from within.

In my experience, as people begin to ponder the possibility of exhaling something they don't want—pain or struggles or stress, for example—two diametrically opposed reactions arise. Some people say, "I can get rid of the things I don't want, like stress or pain? Great!" Others experience a strange sort of guilt or hesitation, as if we are inflicting the world with our unwanted negativity.

Basically, there are two possibilities when we exhale pain or anger or doubt. The first possibility is that this whole thing is symbolic. It is a way to tell the body to relax. Don't let this water down the effectiveness of the practice for you. Symbols are incredibly powerful. But if this is the case, that the entire affair is just a thing in our minds, a way to communicate with our body that runs deeper than words, then, of course, it doesn't really matter what we exhale into the world. On the other hand, it is possible that there is something that is actually, literally happening when we exhale our thoughts into the world. But if this is the case, the negativity, whatever it is, does not belong in us. Returning this thing to the universe outside of us is placing it where it belongs. If we had a kitchen full of smoke, most of us wouldn't hesitate to open the windows. We wouldn't hesitate to "inflict" the smoke on the outside world. We would realize that the outside world is vast. It will be able to handle the intrusion, even if this thing is toxic within our small environment.

We can also envision a neutralizing zone where, once we have sent out negativity, it dissolves seconds after leaving our lips.

Of course, we don't have to limit ourselves to only the inhale or the exhale. When we choose just one part of the breath, however, we are creating an open space, a time of silence with the other part of the breath. If I focus on the words with the inhale, the exhale is my time of silence. Conversely, if I focus on the words with the exhale, the inhale is my time of silence. When we breathe only with one breath-part, we might use that open time to sit in the hopes of not thinking about anything. Sometimes this works.

The time in our meditation that we sit without words, therefore, sometimes acts like a punctuation mark. It is a call for a pause, for quiet. It emphasizes the phrase by surrounding it with silence. We can choose to cultivate this silence by turning our attention to the breath when we are in the "silent" part of the meditation. We might choose, in advance, that during this time we will do our best to release our thoughts entirely.

Lots more will be said in upcoming chapters about doing our best to release our thoughts. For now, let's just resign ourselves to the reality that the mind's job is to think. Therefore, it's wise to be compassionate with ourselves. We will never fully escape our thoughts, so please don't set yourself up for frustration by expecting a time of total thoughtlessness in the silence.

Other times we might use that pause to meditate on the significance of the word that we have just "said." This method of meditating on the meaning of the word is particularly effective when we actually use our vocal cords. If we exhale and say "peace" out loud, we have employed various muscles in the larynx, mouth, and throat, as well as the ears. After the bodily stimulation, we can give the mind a moment to do its thing. We think on that word "peace."

A final option available is to reserve one word for the inhalation, focusing on the things we wish to have more of, and use another word for the exhalation. We might, for example, wish to bring ourselves a more robust sense of love. And so we inhale the word "love." We might wish to rid ourselves of stress. And so we exhale the word "stress." Sometimes, this method feels very powerful for me. Other times, it is a bit too busy, a bit too much.

To review: One basic type of breath prayer has us saying the phrase of our choosing with the inhalation. A second type of breath prayer uses the sacred phrase on the exhalation. A third type employs the phrase on both the inhalation and the exhalation.

Try them all, then reflect on which was your favorite.

One reason to do these practices is that they help us get in touch with the things we believe. That is why this practice is placed here, in the chapter on beliefs. During a time of deconstruction it might be hard to find much that we still hold on to. The good news is that it doesn't take much. Just a phrase or even a single word is enough. And even if you don't fully believe it now, you might choose something you want to believe.

Often, the practice of a breath prayer might renew your feelings about peace, love, or whatever word you chose. Other times, trying on a word or phrase in a breath prayer highlights for us the fact that we really can't endorse those words anymore. It might be that breathing the name "Jesus," for example, helps you come to grips with the fact that Jesus does not have emotional meaning to you now. This may be painful—but it is also helpful. And while this feeling may or may not be a lasting one, it is good to be in touch with where you are right at this moment. No guilt trips necessary.

Whatever word or phrase we choose can be a helpful tool for focusing the mind. It is not generally possible to think about nothing, but it is possible to think about a single thing so intensely that it blots nearly everything out. This occurs in a subtle way with the sorts of breath prayers described above. But it can be used more intentionally.

# An Introduction to Mantra Meditation and Centering Prayer

We now leave the area of breath prayer and move into the realm of mantra. Within some traditions, the word chosen for a mantra has a mystical or metaphysical significance. According to these traditions, there is something inherent to the word or sound chosen that helps the process along. We don't need to have this belief about a mantra before using one. We can use the word or phrase we chose without giving it any special and inherent meaning.

Mantra-based meditation can appear quite similar to breath prayers. Both utilize a single word or phrase to release the focus on more complex and disruptive thoughts. However, there are important differences between a breath prayer and a mantra, and these should not be overlooked.

The most important difference is around the frequency with which the sacred words are used. Breath prayer is like a metronome. The words are used regularly and consistently, regardless of what is happening in the mind. Sometimes this will be with the inhale, other times the exhale. With breath prayers, the point is (at least partially) the words themselves. Breath prayers are a good place to begin for those in spiritual transition. Often, at this time there are not many things we still believe. Breath prayers can help us consolidate our faith in the one or two things we still hold on to.

Mantras, meanwhile, use words as a gateway to transcending words themselves. Mantras are a powerful way to remind ourselves that words are just not that important. When a word is repeated over and over in any context, it soon sounds like nonsense. Mantra meditation takes advantage of this phenomenon. By saying the sounds over and over again, we are reminded that the word itself is not inherently connected to the meaning. There is nothing about the sounds in G–O–D inherent to the Creator of the universe. It is merely a societal agreement, an arbitrary convention. In my experience, this reminds me of the fact that words themselves have limitations, and that there is a reality beyond words.

It is easy to think that all our beliefs are things that can be expressed in words. American students say the Pledge of Allegiance in school every day; Boy Scouts recite their motto; and elected officials, police officers, new citizens, and doctors all recite a promise that is said to encapsulate the most important aspects of the roles they are taking on. Likewise, religious groups have their creeds and commandments, their paths and their pillars. Rituals and holy days often come with expected words meant to be recited. Worship services might be composed of words we say each time we participate. We memorize scripture and sing the words of a song together. All these routines reinforce the idea that we share a system of belief that is best expressed through certain words. We bond ourselves through reciting them together.

As you transition out of the place you are in, as you enter into this liminal space, as you deconstruct and take the descent into your underworld, it is likely that you come to doubt those beliefs that are expressed in words. The fact that you are no longer participating in rituals and routines that elevate these words will likely have an impact.

This might be scary.

This is definitely good for you.

This can be a time to explore those beliefs that don't exist in words. Hold them close. They help this time feel less lonely.

Perhaps you are having resistance to the idea that we can have beliefs that don't exist in words. My experience is that this question reveals a lot about the way we experience our mind working. Some of us just progress with an inner monologue, and our entire cognitive experience is framed with words. Others of us have an experience of the coding of our thoughts into words. Regardless of the way a person is wired, I think the following thought experiment is instructive.

Bring to mind someone you love. Do you believe you love them? Of course you do. Now, if I asked why you loved them, you would probably be able to tell me some wonderful things about that person. But there are wonderful things about other people too. So I might put the question to you again, "But why do you love this particular individual?" Or I could say, "Well, why is that a good reason to love this person?"

I suspect you would probably have a good answer to those second-level questions. Perhaps if I repeated the questions continually, you could go a few more rounds. But I am confident you will reach a place when you say, "Well, my love for this person just is. I know what I know."

There are lots of beliefs you have that do not have words. You know what you know. Some of them are not very healthy or helpful. They are not true. Others are the foundations of the most important things about you.

The temptation at times of transition is to believe that all our beliefs are gone. The reality is that this is not true. *Many* of our beliefs are gone. Most likely the ones that could be expressed with words were the first to go. I don't want to minimize this. It hurts and it is hard. Please give yourself space to mourn those beliefs just as much as you mourn your lost friends or lost opportunities. These beliefs are no small thing. But they are not all our beliefs.

Mantra meditation specifically and contemplative practice in general help us clear away the constant flow of words into our mind. They help us find the things that are more fundamental than words, more basic to who we are.

One way to use a mantra is to think or say the word only when thoughts rise up. It is not, therefore, tied to either the inhalation or the exhalation. It might be used several times per breath. It might be used only a few times every few minutes. The frequency is not important. Using the word and frequently releasing your thoughts does not mean that you are doing it wrong.

This form of meditation is also well loved within the Buddhist tradition. Within a Christian context, this form of meditation is called "centering prayer." Centering prayer consents to the work of the Holy Spirit as a part of the process.

A second approach to using a mantra is to say or think the word constantly. There are many different approaches to this practice. Some suggest following your intuition about whether to change the pitch and speed with which you are saying the word(s). Others call for using the same word at a robotic speed over and over again.

## Practice 4
## Centering Prayer

- *Place your feet flat on the floor.*

- *Consent to whatever work the Holy Spirit would do in you today. (If you are not comfortable thinking in terms of the Holy Spirit, experiment with other word such as the Universe, Light, or Love.)*

- *Sit in a manner that is upright, but not rigid.*

- *Inhale.*

- *Exhale.*

- *Release your worries, stress, and concerns.*

- *Inhale,*

- *Exhale.*

- *As worries, thoughts, and concerns arise, say or think your sacred phrase to release these.*

- *Continue.*

# CHAPTER THREE

❧❧❧❧❧❧❧❧❧❧❧❧❧❧❧❧

# Who Is Left in My Life Now?

There is a long list of unpleasant feelings associated with spiritual transitions. For me, one of the worst is loneliness.

During a transition, we are lonely because we miss the other people who were a part of our lives. As much as this, though, we miss the person we used to be. In this chapter, we explore each of these first two sources of loneliness: our community and ourselves. There is also another form of loneliness. The topic of the loneliness we feel because we are distant from God is such a large topic it will get the entirety of the next chapter.

(A little side note, here, dear readers. I hope you can forgive my constant use of the word "God." I recognize that it might convey a sense that there are not other spiritual realities that are important to people. I intend the word throughout this book as a sort of shorthand, a one-word summing up of whatever it is you believe or had believed in. I think the word is a worthy shorthand not so much because it is inherent to the Christian tradition as it is a rather vague term that can encompass many concepts. If it makes you uncomfortable, however, feel free to substitute another word such as "Light," "Spirit," or "Love.")

## The Loneliness of Losing Our Community

The loneliness we feel because of missing our community might begin with a simple, obvious fact: we are not very often seeing the people who were once like a second family. For many of us, our involvement with church was more than a weekly worship service. It might have been additional formal/official or informal/unofficial gatherings. It might have been in-person meet-ups and texts or phone calls and e-mails. Maybe it was just the knowledge that these people were out there for us. Perhaps now we look at the wasteland our social calendar has become and feel something like anxiety. When we do see old friends from our church, at best we have less in common; at worst, insinuations about the journey we are on go unsaid—but not unthought—by the other people.

Many times we will encounter worry related to our leaving. Sometimes it is quite obvious and out in the open. The people within the old community fear that we have "back-slidden," that our souls are now endangered. It's better if they can say what they're thinking: "You are becoming one of them." Other times we wonder where we stand with our once-friends. All we know for sure is that things are different now.

One of the signs of a mature faith is the ability to see past the obvious, surface-layer meaning of things. As we long to discover the essence, we learn to go deeper than taking things at face value. Recall that this is almost the definition of deconstruction. We begin to see the elements of things for what they really are. This basic principle manifests itself in so many ways. But one of the first is the idea that what people say may not be connected to what they really believe.

Let's be blunt here: the members of that community might even think they believe what they say about their faith. But in fact, they may be deluding themselves.

When the people we once cared for say things that surprise and hurt us; when the people from our old communities try to "rescue" us; when they don't return our phone calls; when they make it clear that everything is different now. . . in all these cases, it appears that their words and actions are about us. The people with whom we were once in community tell themselves and everyone around them that they desire only for us to be better, safer, happier.

But often that isn't the case at all.

My hope for you is that the community from which you are transitioning is a healthy one. Perhaps that season in your life has run its course. Maybe you are ready to find yourself moving on. Maybe the people within that group are comfortable enough with whom they are to be at peace with your leaving.

But for many of us, it doesn't work that way. And even in the healthiest groups, there is some unhealthiness going on. It might be subtle. It might be profound. Somewhere, in almost every group, there is energy invested in determining what the group is and what the group is not.

In this act of defining, psychological processes are going on. When we put ourselves inside a certain circle and we put others outside that circle, the "other" becomes so much more than a collection of people who did not make the cut. On the surface, it can appear that a line between who is in and who is out divides two groups of people from one another. "They don't look like us . . . talk like us . . . dress like us . . . vote like us . . . believe like us." Often, though, it is not about division between two groups at all. Even when it appears that it is.

Human beings are complicated. We all have ways we don't mesh with the group we want to belong to, and if we want to belong to the group desperately enough, we might subjugate whatever elements of ourselves don't fit. We then have to figure out what to do with the feelings, desires, and parts of our personalities that are not allowed. At its worst and ugliest, this becomes the pastor who sermonizes every week about the uncontrolled sexuality of this generation while he is having an affair. This becomes the deacon who leads the homophobic crusade in the church while she pushes down her own sexual identity. This becomes the church leader who tells everyone he is terrified of the Muslims coming to steal his job, while he is stealing from his own company.

Those of us who work at being honest with ourselves hopefully avoid those extremes. Most of us do not engage in such obviously dysfunctional behavior. But all of us do have things within us that we try to put outside of us. We can't make the feelings go away. So we convince ourselves the unwelcome feelings and ideas belong to someone else. They become personified in the flesh of the people who had already been out there, beyond the confines of our cozy little crowd.

This is why in a community with a clear in-group and out-group, one of the key fixations is so often a fear of doubt. Any hesitation or "lack of faith" is a sign of weakness. The problem is, however, that every single person has fears and doubts. None of us have faith in all the things we are expected to, all the time. But the people on the inside, who receive messages over and over again that a lack of faith is not allowed, project their fears outside.

This is less prevalent in healthier groups. The transition from a healthier group might be easier in many ways. But projection, in-groups and out-groups—they are nearly always a dynamic as members leave a group. And in those groups where it is less obvious it may also be much more infuriating to identify and pin down. It can be more difficult to see and name and combat.

The loneliness of leaving a spiritual community often comes as a surprise to the person leaving. We didn't expect it was going to be this bad. We didn't expect that the people would be this mean. We didn't imagine it was going to be that easy for others to let us go.

There's some comfort to be found in this: it's not about you. It's not about me. The people in your community who think they are talking to you, who appear to be talking to you—they are really talking to the parts of themselves they cannot own.

When we leave a community we are not only taking a journey from inside a church to the outside of it. We are traveling from the world of the people the community knows to the world of the people the community only imagines. The things that they imagine are not always very nice.

Of course it is not always so obvious. In some cases, nobody says anything at all. This brings with it its own batch of hurts and surprises. But there are two things worth noticing when we leave a group and are greeted by nothing but the chirping of crickets. The first thing is that it really can be a no-win situation for the people we are leaving behind. They may not know if—and what—they should tell us about how they feel around the issues of us and our leaving. The very fact of their silence testifies to the mix of boundaries and emotions, the presence of projection and other subconscious mechanisms.

All the thinking in the world doesn't help a whole lot, though. Understanding of the why only goes so far. Regardless of why these things happen, they hurt.

This is one of the lessons of deconstruction. I once believed there was a formula. I once believed there was a list of things that you said or believed that would significantly change difficult times. Now, I know that you get through it. Pain is part of the process. It is hard. There might be some paths that are easier than others. But there are no paths that are easy. There is no black-and-white prescription that bypasses the difficult things.

Those lists of pat responses, the party line—they had their value to insiders. It isn't only in the words themselves. When I was hurting before, and somebody provided the "official" response to the kind of pain or hurt I was experiencing, it reminded us both that we belonged to that group. It was like performing a secret handshake, or saying the Scout's motto. When I believed that group was enough for me, this reminder was sometimes welcome.

As we walk away from the group, the words they say can seem hurtful and shallow. We wonder why they were ever comforting. It might be helpful to remind ourselves: the comfort was never truly about the words themselves. It was always about what those words signified.

A spiritual exercise would be helpful, now, I think. The practice that follows is one that sprang up out of the centering-prayer tradition. Recall that centering prayer was explored in practice 4. As intrusive thoughts arise, we might dismiss them with a sacred word. You might begin your time with practice 5 and then transition into centering prayer. Or you might practice this exercise independently.

## Practice 5
## A Welcoming Prayer

- *Create a safe, quiet environment for yourself. Turn down your phone and consider lighting a candle.*

- *Breathe deeply in through the nose and out through the mouth.*

- *Take a mental inventory of where you are, right now. List the feelings you are experiencing. Do your best to engage this with a nonjudgmental attitude. Your feelings are neither good nor bad. They simply are.*

- *Choose the feeling that seems to be the most impactful. Think, or say*

*"Welcome, _____." (For example, "Welcome, fear"; "Welcome, sadness"; "Welcome, anxiety"; etc.)*

- *Inhale. Exhale.*
- *Say or think, "I let go of my desire for security and survival."*
- *Inhale. Exhale.*
- *Say or think, "I let go of my desire for esteem and affection."*
- *Breathe again.*
- *Say or think, "I let go of my desire for power and control."*
- *Breathe.*
- *Say or think, "I let go of my desire to change the situation."*

*If you wish, you can repeat this process to welcome as many feelings as you are carrying.*

## The Loneliness of Losing the Person We Used to Be

When I realized that the things my community was saying and doing weren't about me at all, I felt so free. It was quite wonderful. In fact, it went too far, beyond my simply not taking it personally. It was more than being able to say, "The things you are saying or doing, and the ways that you are ignoring me—you are really saying and doing these things to the parts of yourself that you do not wish to own." Instead, I had, in truth, a sense of self-righteousness. A bit of arrogance and superiority.

And then it hit me. Projection is not a one-sided event. I have my own fears and worries. For example, there was the nagging doubt: *What if they are right? What if hell works the way they say it does? What if this deconstruction is caused by something wrong with me, just like they believe?*

I didn't think they loomed particularly large, these fears of mine. But they were distressing to entertain. So I didn't let myself entertain them for very long. And so this all leads to the questions: Did I have these fears under control in a mostly healthy way? Or did they seem so small because I was busy projecting them elsewhere?

I was not aware of the fact that I was doing some mental accounting. Deep within, I was considering something: If this community I had once belonged to was composed of wonderful people worth listening to, then those insecurities of mine had merit. If this community was composed of unreflective, angry, emotionally stunted knuckle-heads, then those concerns of mine became easy to dismiss.

In short, I had a vested interest in embarking on an internal smear campaign. To the extent that this campaign was successful in my own mind, I felt better about leaving, but I felt so much more alone. I wondered who I was back then, that I could ever have seen these people in a positive light. I was tempted to distrust my own intuitions and instincts. I told myself that these had led me astray in choosing that community.

I can see now that at the time I chose that community, it was the right thing for me. And the time I left the community? That also was the right thing to do in those circumstances. It was time. Making that community the culprit made it easier to go, in many ways. In seeing them as so different from whom I had become, I realized how far I had traveled. I realized I was not the same person I had once been. And I didn't know this new me very well.

Maybe your story is like my story.

I suspect that you have changed a lot. I did, and the story I needed to tell myself at that time was that I had changed so much I hardly recognized myself anymore. I had to put all my fears and insecurities somewhere. So I scapegoated that group, much like they had done to me. This awareness hurts.

Many times in our lives we have to live in denial of our insecurities. If we did not, we would be paralyzed. And then, certainly, all would be lost. If you are anything like me, you had to put those insecurities somewhere or you would have never left, so maybe you located them right on the people to whom you were once so close.

It's worth emphasizing that none of this means that the old community was good for us then or now. None of this means that what was said or done was fair or reasonable. There are powerful differences between yourself and this group. But in order to make it make sense that we ever belonged in that group at all, we are forced to carry the fact that we have changed so much that we don't even know who we are anymore.

One part of loneliness is the feeling that we have lost the selves we once knew. We used to be a certain person. That person had certain ways of being in the world. Some of those ways go away when we leave a belief system. Back then, we didn't have to discover a solution every time things got confusing in life. We had a go-to response, a pattern of ways to respond and to understand the situation. When we begin a transition, we lose some of those robotic responses and are forced to grapple with new, more genuine ones.

That hurts, but pain won't destroy us. It's just that annoying dog barking away at the cars that are driving by. And I don't know of anything better at helping a person to sit with their hurts than a contemplative practice.

This is why the welcoming prayer can help us. Naming the emotions we are feeling, and welcoming them, is valuable. So is putting them in perspective.

When I am angry, I come to identify myself with my anger. When I am hurt—whether it is a physical or emotional pain—I see little of myself beyond that pain. Perhaps most to our point here, when I am lonely, I come to think that I am the loneliness itself. When I am suffering, I see so little of myself beyond that suffering.

It became natural, then, to wish to disconnect myself from the suffering by distracting myself. If I just didn't think about the loneliness, I figured, I would remember that there is more to me than just that.

This doesn't often work for me. Does it work for you?

Contemplation has taught me to dwell in my suffering. Not forever. Not even for an hour. But for a while. A few minutes. Half an hour, maybe.

Even something physical, like a headache, needs to be acknowledged.

When I stop running from that hurt and spend a moment occupying that space, I usually discover two things quite quickly. The first thing I discover is that when I turn off all my distractions, all my attempts to ignore my pain, what I feel is not as bad as I thought it would be. I suspect the energy I put into trying to shield myself from this makes it worse, not better. The second thing I discover is that even if the suffering was intense, it is just suffering. It doesn't kill me to experience it.

I am reminded that I am not my suffering, that this suffering is only an experience I am having, because I have enlisted something that can stand over the loneliness and behold it. I can watch my suffering with interested compassion, and in doing that, I learn that I am so much more than my suffering.

As we set out on our journey of transition, many of us begin with grand abstractions. One part of the contemplative journey is to learn to dwell in the specific and concrete reality where we find ourselves. I explore more than study my suffering and transform it from a general abstraction into a particular lived reality. Not just back pain, but this particular back pain. Not just loneliness, but this particular loneliness I am feeling right now. We learn to be present to this particular moment. We learn to name this specific feeling. We come to attend to this particular hurt.

In this spirit of moving out of the abstract and toward the specific, let me share a few final suggestions around the idea of navigating the loneliness that comes up in spiritual transitions.

Do your best to treat yourself and others with grace, kindness, and good humor. Give people an opportunity or two to surprise you pleasantly. If you can, tell them where you are coming from.

But if you can't? If things are not working out? Then it's time to decide where your boundaries are. When I am worried about difficult interactions, I sometimes even plan out in advance a very simple phrase of what I am going to expect of the people around me.

For example, if I am trying to have lunch with someone but I am not wanting to discuss heaven and hell with them, I will say, "I am not ready to talk about that right now."

If they attempt to do this, I will repeat. "I am not ready to talk about that right now."

And when it goes into a third time I begin with my statement and add a very simple phrase to it. "I am not ready to talk about that right now, and if you continue I am going to need to leave."

This brief statement is all about me. It is about my feelings and what I am prepared to do. There is a part of me not comfortable with this; after all, we are told to be considerate of others. But this is a time to take care of myself. It is a time to work out whether a relationship with these once-friends is going to work.

I have found that when I try to sound happy, it just seems weird and fake and kind of Stepford Wives–ish. So I go for simply not having much emotion in my voice at all. My goal is to be just a little bit quieter than the other person. I don't want to seem insecure, but I also don't want to escalate the situation.

None of this is easy or fun. I am tempted to be loud. I want to engage them in a debate. Maybe someday I will. But not today.

There are some people from whom I may need some distance. Many of us, I suspect, tend to underestimate the importance of creating this important boundary. Most of us err on the side of trying to maintain relationships even during the time of transition. It's worth doing some hard work on this. As we experience that temptation to maintain old friendships, consider some questions: What's our motivation? Why are we doing this? Is this coming from a desire to spread love? Is it coming out of a fear of rocking the boat? Is it coming from suffering that I have not yet faced and named quite specifically, which therefore feels too extraordinary to bear?

Going through this period of time without these once-allies is not easy. Loneliness is a real thing, felt in the body. But doing this time well is an investment that pays off.

In some cases, when the hurts (probably on both sides) are not so fresh, relationships might be easier to resume. In other cases, the perspective of time helps us to see that a relationship was not what we thought it was when we were in the middle of it.

A Buddhist practice is one of the things I have found that helps me to work through these challenges with former close friends.

Buddhist? I suspect there are some readers who read that word and have no major reaction at all. But for others, this very moment might be a crossroads. This could be a pretty big deal. Sometimes, there are negative attitudes toward other spiritual traditions within spiritual communities. Even if we rationally know that this is not a healthy feeling, we might have trouble overcoming our indoctrination. My experience as a contemplative and mystic has confirmed my intuition that there is a lot of wisdom all over the world. Over and over again, I live the reality that our particular words and ideas are so flimsy and inadequate. I do not see how any single religion could corner the market on the Divine.

Buddhism, in particular, possesses very useful tools. Historically, this tradition did a much better job than my native Christianity at honoring spiritual practices and continuing to promote their use across many sects and denominations. Buddhism's riches do not replace my Christian beliefs; rather, they enhance them.

Perhaps, though, you aren't there. That is okay. Following practice 6, which is my best attempt to express a traditional Buddhist practice, is a modified version. Though the overarching format owes something to Buddhist thought, the words I use are from a traditional Irish Christian blessing. If beginning with the traditional Buddhist form is not comfortable right now, I would encourage you to give the modified version a try.

Regardless of which of these two practices you try, you are going to need to have at least three people in mind before you begin these practices. The first is someone you love very much, such as a spouse or child. The second is someone for whom you experience ambivalence or neutral feeling, such as a coworker you don't know very well. The third person to bring to mind is someone with whom you struggle, perhaps someone from the spiritual community you are leaving.

# Practice 6
## Loving-Kindness Meditation

- *Sit comfortably.*

- *Take three deep breaths: inhalations and exhalations.*

- *Now bring to mind the person whom you love most. See them in your mind's eye in an outfit they would be likely wear. Hear their voice. Bring to mind any scents or other sensations you might associate with them.*

- *With your next inhale, think or say, "May you be healthy." Exhale.*

- *With your next inhale, think or say, "May you be happy." Exhale.*

- *With your next inhale, think or say, "May you be free." Exhale.*

- *Inhale. Exhale.*

- *Bring to mind the person to whom you feel neutral or ambivalent. See them with as many senses as possible.*

- *With your next inhale, think or say, "May you be healthy." Exhale.*

- *With your next inhale, think or say, "May you be happy." Exhale.*

- *With your next inhale, think or say, "May you be free." Exhale.*

- *Inhale. Exhale.*

- *Now, bring to mind that person with whom you struggle. Try to experience them vividly in your mind. Be an interested observer to any feelings this brings up in you.*

- *With your next inhale, think or say, "May you be healthy." Exhale.*

- *With your next inhale, think or say, "May you be happy." Exhale.*

- *With your next inhale, think or say, "May you be free." Exhale.*

- *Inhale. Exhale.*

- *Now, it is time for you. See yourself in your mind's eye. It might be helpful to try to see yourself through the eyes of the person on whom you first focused.*

*Or make an attempt at seeing yourself through God's eyes.*

- *With your next inhale, think or say, "May I be healthy." Exhale.*

- *With your next inhale, think or say, "May I be happy." Exhale.*

- *With your next inhale, think or say, "May I be free." Exhale.*

- *Inhale. Exhale.*

## Practice 7
## An Irish Blessing

- *Create a calm and quiet space; turn off your phone and do your best to assure yourself of uninterrupted time.*

- *For the duration of this exercise, give yourself permission to be free of the duties and obligations to which you normally submit yourself.*

- *For a minute or two, simply breathe:*

*in through the nose, and out through the mouth.*

- *Think of a person for whom you feel gratitude. (Choose a single person to focus on. Don't worry; you will have an opportunity to focus on others shortly.)*

- *Inhale and bring their appearance to your mind. Try to hear their voice, and even smell their unique scent. Feel, as best you can, their presence. Exhale.*

- *For the duration of a breath, allow yourself to experience whatever feelings this person stirs within you at this moment.*

- *With your next inhale, think to this person: "May the road rise up to meet you."*

- *Exhale.*

- *With your next inhale, think to this person: "May the wind be always at your back."*

- *Exhale.*

- *With your next inhale, think: "May the sun shine warm on your face."*

- *Exhale.*

- *With your next inhale, think: "May the rains fall softly on your fields."*

- *Exhale.*

- *With the next inhale, think: "May you be held in the palm of God's hand."*

- *For the next breath, rejoice in the thought that your friend would be experiencing all these things.*

- *If you have more time, move on to another person for whom you feel grateful. If you are having trouble choosing, consider these questions: Who are you grateful for in your home? Who are you grateful for in your school or workplace? Who are you thankful for in your social circles? Who are you thankful for from your past? Who are you thankful for in your present? Are there people who took on a role of parent, sibling, boss, coworker, lover, friend,*

*coach, leader, follower for whom you
are thankful? People who shaped you
personally, professionally, or spiritu-
ally? Whoever you choose, the phrases
to focus on are these:
May the road rise up to meet you.
May the wind be always at your back.
May the sun shine warm upon your face.
May the rains fall soft upon your fields.
May you be held in the palm of
   God's hand.*

- *When you are ready to conclude
today's practice, take a single, cleansing breath.*

- *Now, with your inhale, think this
for yourself: "May the road rise up to
meet me."*

- *Exhale.*

- *With your inhale: "May the wind be
always at my back."*

- *Exhale.*

- *With your inhale: "May the sun shine
warm upon my face."*

- *Exhale.*
- *Inhale, think: "May the rains fall soft upon my fields."*
- *Exhale.*
- *Inhale, think: "May I be held in the palm of God's hand."*

One of the things I found when I left my spiritual community was that I was not very interested in praying the way I always had before. Petitionary prayer—talking to God in my mind and asking for things—was just about the only contemplative practice in which we engaged. I associated it with that community, and I was beginning to doubt that God actually worked that way at all. The loss of this practice led to my loneliness from God (which we will explore in the next chapter). But it also led to a loneliness from the community of which I had been a part. Praying for dear friends had always helped me to feel closer to them. The fact that I had difficulty doing it, when I once had found it so easy, reinforced my sense of isolation and loneliness.

Loving-kindness meditation (and the more Christianized variant described in practice 7) gave me a replacement. It helped the loneliness I felt; it was a salve to treat the alienation from the people I had once loved, alienation from the person I once was, and the loneliness I felt, disconnected from God. It was one of the foundations of a spiritual practice that grew to be much richer than the single option I had once had.

For the rest of this book, there will be at least two spiritual practices presented in almost every chapter. When all is said and done you will have explored more than thirty different practices. Maybe you will never do any of them again, and that's okay. But you might benefit from making these practices part of your life.

My experience tells me that investing between fifteen and sixty minutes a day, in one or two separate sessions, can be life-changing. Mainstream, peer-reviewed science backs this up. I have found that going through a period of casually "dating" lots of practices before making a more serious commitment to a few is a smart way to go. As you work toward this goal, I suspect it will be good for you to keep going back to the ones you like as you build a regular routine.

But I could be wrong. I think maybe not enough people are willing to say that. Those who are sure they have the answers for everybody else have done quite a lot of damage. Let's agree to operate from the premise that as adults we are pretty good at figuring out what we need. I can offer you some suggestions to try. But trust your own intuition about what will work best for you.

Somewhere along your spiritual transition, you might find yourself struggling to trust your own voice. This is a sad, sad thing. More than anything else, I hope, dear friend, that you feel confident in knowing what you know, loving what you love, trusting in the things you think you want for yourself.

Therefore, I hope you will take my suggestions with a grain of salt. The sky's the limit. You get to decide. The question isn't "What should you do with all these practices?" The question is "What would you like to do with them?"

# CHAPTER FOUR

# My God, Why Have You Forsaken Me?

One of the big struggles during these times is that we discover God is not whom we thought. We find ourselves connecting with the image of the crucified Jesus, who said, "My God, why have you forsaken me?"

It might be that we no longer sense a connection with the Divine because we do not feel comfortable or welcomed engaging in all those practices that once brought us closer to God. It might be that suddenly we are doubting some things we never allowed ourselves to doubt before. We might find ourselves wondering if God even exists at all.

# Beliefs About God

Our beliefs about God are tricky. If we were thinking about pursuing a different career or taking up a new hobby, we could talk about these in a lot of different aspects of our lives. But ideas about God? Once we lose our spiritual community, there are not many places we can share our thoughts about what this is like.

Our beliefs about God are further complicated because the sorts of things that count as evidence are different here. As we explore our beliefs and loneliness related to our community, it is clear enough who that community is and what they are doing. As we explore our beliefs and loneliness about ourselves, we can know what we feel and what we are doing, even if we don't completely recognize ourselves. But we can't pin God down on an examining table. Our knowledge of God is less direct. We don't see, hear, or touch God directly.

The things we understand about God become the ways we land our new beliefs. Since we may not have anyone right now who is helping us to work out what the real options are, it is natural to default to what we believed before. It's easy to miss the startling variety of options available to us. Here are just a few examples.

You can become an angry and militant atheist who picks fights on the Internet. Or you can become someone who doesn't believe in God but finds elements of spirituality marvelous. You can become a "New Ager" who arms yourself with crystals and a variety of religious traditions—or a down-to-earth journeyer who sees wisdom in many different directions. You can become a fire-and-brimstone Baptist who starts imitating a Southern accent or you can join a Baptist church and feel it build the love within you.

When we were in our spiritual communities, life may have seemed like a true-and-false test. As we step out of these places, we might begin to see our options as multiple choice. The reality is so much bigger than we thought. And the exam isn't mandatory; you can choose to crumple up the assessment, throw it in the trash can, and walk out of class.

There is a tremendous amount of choice in what we can believe. We can dress this up in a variety of ways, but it does not change a basic fact: to an extent, you and everyone around you have chosen what you believe. You are doing it right now. You will do it again.

Perhaps our growing and changing beliefs are so huge that calling this supernatural force by the same name doesn't even make sense anymore. Maybe you don't think about "God" any-more. Some people find it helpful to begin to think about "Spirit" or "The Universe" or "Mother." This can be a useful way to remind ourselves of the new things we are learning.

Others find themselves in a space of not believing that there is anything beyond them. Countless shades of meaning, nuance, and options are available. There are lots of good reasons to think that the act of believing in God has been a destructive tendency in humanity. There are also lots of reasons to think that the entity we called God is really just a kind of shorthand for what is best about people. And there are lots of reasons to think that all these names do, in fact, point at something beyond us.

My goal here is to not to provide a comprehen-sive analysis of all these options. The people who actually carry these beliefs could do them justice better than I can. For our purposes here, I am interested in witnessing and naming the difficulty of this process. It is hard and it hurts. I am also interested in providing some reminders that there is much freedom here, and even some things to cel-ebrate. In this strange, sad, wonderful time, build-ing your spiritual practice will make it easier.

These considerations do not mean that every-body just makes everything up as they go. If we chose to have the belief that every rainbow has a pot of gold at its end, we would not be able to realistically act on this belief. Life would quickly make it very difficult, even impossible, to sustain this idea.

There are other sorts of beliefs, though, that are much more difficult for life to confirm or deny. These beliefs can be nurtured, or they can be fought against. The way we do this is through the way we live. It's the ideas we have and the choices we make. The thoughts we choose to focus on. The way we construct our spiritual practice.

This sense of loneliness rooted in no longer knowing who God is will fade. Sometimes it will fade because the not-knowing becomes safe and comfortable. But that is not the only end game.

Other times after a spiritual transition, the loneliness begins to fade because a new picture begins to form. We have some choice in the matter. Every day will be built on the decisions that we will get to make for ourselves. We will come closer to certain destinations. We will go further away from others.

Spiritual communities are often criticized for focusing so much on orthodoxy (right belief), while there is little talk of orthopraxy (right practice). Personally, I thought that beliefs were the only way I would know God. Back when I was a philosophy student, I was very interested in constructing elaborate towers out of my beliefs. When I was an evangelical, I was interested in studying the ways others constructed theirs. But the knowledge we come to in this abstract way is only one way to know. Another is going out to do, to be in the world. We come to know God in the doing of good things. There is much mature religious wisdom about entering into the world's suffering. It is a path to alleviate the loneliness we feel when we feel separated from God.

It is worth repeating that the power of building your spiritual practice now is that it also can (if you want it to) help maintain some of that closeness to God. You might even have experiences as you try these practices that bring you to new understandings and conclusions.

The first practice we will try out in this chapter is another breath prayer (like practice 3). The practices presented as 8, 9, and 10 are interconnected. It might be that only one of them resonates with where you are at this time. They also can be tried as a progression. They could be done one at a time, across several sessions, or a few minutes might be devoted to each during the same time of silence.

The first two of these breath prayers revolve around the questions "Who are you, God?" and

"Who am I, God?" I do not recommend trying to provide an answer to either question. My experience with these two questions is that this time is best spent sitting in the tension of not having answers. As you ask the questions and things arise, I encourage you to return your focus to your breath.

In addition to committing for a certain length of time, I would like to encourage you to eliminate as many of the distractions that you can. I used to tell myself that I was meditating while I would use a timer on my laptop, and I would often leave a social media page wide open while I did it. I would begin my practice and whenever I got those delicious chimes telling me that something was happening on my social media platform, I had two choices. One was to wonder what was going on, in which case the session was diminished because some of my attention was now turned to the social media page. The other choice was to interrupt my session and check the alert, in which case there was still a loss in what I would otherwise have reaped from the session. Perhaps you are better at resisting this temptation. But are there other preoccupations and distractions that might intrude on your time? Are there any reasonable steps you might take to minimize these?

# Practice 8
# Who Am I?

- *Inhale.*

- *Exhale.*

- *Inhale.*

- *Exhale.*

- *Inhale.*

- *Exhale.*

- *With your next inhale, think or say the question, "Who am I, God?"*

- *Exhale.*

- *With your next inhale, think or say, "Who are you, God?"*

- *Devote most of the time you have given to yourself for this practice to asking the questions.*

- *When you are ready, release these questions. Sit in a time of wordless union. If you wish, mentally explore your possible answers to these two questions.*

# Practice 9
## Questions and Answers

- *Inhale.*

- *Exhale.*

- *Inhale.*

- *Exhale.*

- *Inhale.*

- *Exhale.*

- *With your next inhale, think or say the question, "Who am I, God?"*

- *Exhale.*

- *With your next inhale, think or say, "Who are you, God?"*

- *Exhale.*

- *With your next inhale, think or say, "Here I am, God."*

- *Exhale.*

- *With your next inhale, think or say, "Here you are, God."*

- *Devote most of the time you have given to yourself for this practice to asking the questions.*

- *When you are ready, release these questions and make the concluding statements. Sit in a time of wordless union. If you wish, mentally explore your possible answers to these two questions.*

---

# Practice 10
## Questions and Answers

- *Inhale.*

- *Exhale.*

- *Inhale.*

- *Exhale.*

- *Inhale.*

- *Exhale.*

- *With your next inhale, think or say, "Here I am, God."*

- *Exhale.*

- *With your next inhale, think or say, "Here you are, God."*

- *Exhale.*

- *With your next inhale, think or say, "Here we are together."*

- *Devote most of the time you have given to yourself for this practice to making the statements.*

- *When you are ready, release these statements. Sit in a time of wordless union.*

## Breath Prayers 102

These spiritual practices are yours to do as you see fit. Please don't just accept them whole-hog. View them not as rituals handed down verbatim from heaven, but instead, treat them like a recipe discovered online: Change them to fit your needs and situation. Play with them. Tweak them a bit. Explore variations and alterations. Combine them together in some new way. Pull them apart and practice only the portions that work for you.

(Recall that chapter 2 explored the implications of altering the breath during breath prayers.)

Let's explore a few details of breath prayers and some of the more obvious ways to change them. Breath is meditation's most basic building block. It is the place where we begin. Significant changes in the nature of these practices, therefore, can be made by changing the way we breathe with them.

For example, most of the time, we might say or think whatever words on which we are focused with the inhale. This is as good a place as any to begin. When we bring a new thought into our body with the breath, there is a sense of wanting to literally take that idea into our body. With the inhalation, words feel in some sense received.

One way to change a meditation is to change the timing of the words. For example, if we had been thinking of something with the inhalation, we might now say it on the exhalation. Words said with the exhalation begin with the air itself inside of us, but these soon become our gift to the world when we breathe out and send them into the world outside.

Meditations can also vary based on how frequently they call on us to use the phrase. Practices 8, 9, and 10 were written with a lot of openness. They begin with three full breaths and then leave the exhale empty. If words are attached to every inhalation and every exhalation, the practice can feel busier. This busyness has both a positive and a negative side.

The breath itself is a sort of metaphor that looks straightforward but is actually very complex. Similarly, belief in God can seem the same way. There might have been people in our previous faith community who had a vested interest in painting things quite simply: "You can believe like me, or you can believe wrong." Perhaps they believed they were speaking the truth.

## Making Room for Questions

We begin now to move into a territory that might be helpful for some people in spiritual transition. It might be really hard for others.

You do not have to believe in God.

You never had to believe in God.

Those two powerful questions in the preceding practices were inspired by Saint Francis. It is said that he passed an entire night asking those two simple questions: Who are you, God? Who am I, God? There are many people who would have us rush through to the answers. There is power and wisdom in sitting with these questions.

This might be a season where you are trying to work all that out. There are some parts and times in this process where it is best for you to just work through this on your own. If that is where you are now, please, go to the next chapter.

If it is not hard for you to read about God right now, please, by all means, continue.

## God and Breath

Believing in God—like using the breath—is a complex thing. There is, in fact, a long history of connection between God and the breath. In many languages, including ancient Hebrew, the word for "breath" is the same as the word for "Spirit."

The Genesis story even begins with God reaching down, grabbing a handful of earth, and breathing into it. It seems to me that this is where humanity receives the image of God—with the breath of God.

A handful of spiritual practices rose out of this story. We will have to pursue the God–breath connection a little further to make sense out of one of my favorite spiritual practices. It is one we will use to close out the chapter.

In the Bible, God eventually identifies with the letters "YHWH," which are known as the Divine tetragrammaton. Those who translate these words will often render them as "I am what I am" or "I will be what I will be." They can also be translated as the "Living One" or the "Life Giver." We begin, then, with a return to the idea we explored early in this chapter: the very nature of God defies our categories, labels, and words.

Sometimes, these letters are translated "Yahweh." But Jews recognize the foolishness of trying to name God. Many refuse to say this name out loud. The word "Lord" was substituted in English translations for YHWH, but this points us away from the concept of life and breath, and instead implies a hierarchical authoritarian relationship.

Some people go so far as writing "G-d." Personally, I love the mystery in the middle. I love the recognition that we can never fully know God. This humility can feel like a breath of fresh air for those of us who are departing communities where they believed they knew the nature of God much better than those around them.

Many rabbis believe that YHWH was, in fact, never meant to be said at all. They note that there is something unique happening with the things that these sounds do to the mouth and throat. These specific letters, in fact, emulate the act of breathing itself.

If this understanding is right, then the bottom line is that we cannot say God's name in the same way we would name our neighbor or a new type of flower. God is, in a sense, too far away, too alien, too fundamental to the nature of the universe, for this to be a possibility. G-d does not belong to the category of things to which we give word-sound names.

And yet, in that act of breathing, we say God's name hundreds of times each day. It was the first thing we did when we were born. It will be the last thing we do before we die. We say God's name slowly in times of calm. We chant God's name quickly, desperately, in times of panic or ecstasy.

# Practice II
# God's Name

- *Create a space of quiet and safety for yourself by turning off your phone and making the temperature comfortable. Consider getting yourself a glass of water and turning on soft, wordless music.*

- *Place your feet flat on the floor. Inhale slowly through your nose. Exhale slowly through your mouth.*

- *Place your hand on your abdomen.*

*Feel your belly rise and fall as you continue with your breaths.*

- *Spend as long as you wish simply enjoying the act of calmly breathing.*

- *When you are ready, see that the exhale is similar to the first syllable of the translation of God's name "Yah."*

- *See the inhale as related to the second syllable, "Weh."*

- *Continue to breathe, seeing each breath as a pronouncement of God's name, a name more intimate than any sounds can be.*

- *Continue this act of breathing as a saying of God's name for most of the time you had set aside for your practice today.*

- *When you are ready, release your conscious thoughts about saying God's name. Enjoy a time of union.*

- *Throughout your day today, return to your breath, seeing each breath as a calling out to the Creator of the universe.*

We began this chapter contending with the reality that during a spiritual transition, the question, "God, why have you forsaken me?" has a special sort of resonance. At these times, we feel the loneliness implicit in these words in a way that we never have before. There is no bypassing this loneliness, no short circuiting, no positive spin or happy reframe here.

But there is a future for us. A time lies ahead when the loneliness might begin to feel like something else. It might even be something pleasant.

It is hard to see this. When we are in the middle of a certain type of spirituality, we might expect that all beliefs are defined by the ability to express these beliefs. If a belief can't be put into words, it is easy to think it must not be a belief at all.

Sometimes, our inability to express our belief in words is not because our beliefs are missing something. It might be that our beliefs are so profound that no words can properly capture them. It might be that no words adequately express the fullness of the things we know to be true. Recognizing the possibility that God's truest name might be the breath itself is an introduction to this idea, where a lack of words is not an expression of missing something, but rather, is an expression of knowing something fully.

# CHAPTER FIVE

❧❧❧❧❧❧❧❧❧❧❧❧❧❧❧❧

# How Do My Beliefs Work Now?

Oftentimes the best way to truly get at the truth is in an apparent contradiction. Sometimes reality is so complex that the most accurate description we might offer is to proclaim a thing and also proclaim its opposite. Charles Dickens' famous opening, "It was the best of times, it was the worst of times" has become a cliché, but the reason it reached this status is because it offered a deep, resonating description. I think most of us have had parts of our lives that could also be described that way.

Despite the usefulness of paradox, we are so often encouraged to simply "pick one." We are asked to weigh the two possibilities together. Let them fight it out in some sort of mental wrestling ring and declare one of those positions the winner.

## Making Room for Paradox

I would like to invite you into affirming both sides of an apparent contradiction. For example: *Our spiritual background was terrible. Our spiritual background got us to where we are today. God exists. God does not exist. Republicans are right. Democrats are right.*

There is a part of our brain that wants to choose between these incompatible possibilities. They can't both be true, we tell ourselves. Often, this instinct to choose is a good thing. Sometimes we need to decide what is going to happen next. A restaurant server, for example, would like to know which meal we want to order. Our prospective employer would like to know if we are taking the job. Our future spouse would like to know if we plan to show up to the wedding.

The part of our mind that chooses between either/or is known as the dualistic mind. This part of our mind gets so much work it sometimes doesn't think there is anything else. And yet, we saw in the last chapter, that God is so distant that we cannot say God's name. Also, God is so close that we say the Divine name with every breath.

It is likely that you are looking at the place from which you are coming, and thinking that it was terrible. And perhaps at the same time there are things from that time for which you are thankful.

There is wisdom, oftentimes, in rejecting the either/or.

## The Process of Deconstruction

Spiritual deconstruction is a weird thing. It happens, for most of us, in stages. When I ditched my old beliefs, I thought I was deconstructed. I didn't realize that changing the content of my beliefs was just a first step. It was an important first step. It was a necessary first step. But it was only my first one. As I took it, I thought it would be the last. I am so glad it was not.

Permit me a metaphor: it is as if I had been drinking cola from a red Solo cup, while I inhabited that important spiritual community. The first step was dumping out what remained of the cola. I then filled the cup with root beer. There are differences. But not really that many. Eventually I threw the cup into the recycle bin. And I found the waterfall. I walked under it and drank the water right up.

Once I thought the specific beliefs I held were the most important thing. I thought that choosing Coke over root beer was the decision I had to make. I thought changing soda flavors was going to be the whole of it. What I found was that this change was not nearly as big as it seemed, and that much bigger changes were coming.

My first step was to change the content of the beliefs I held. But when I came up against the people who disagreed with these new beliefs, for example, I treated them exactly as I treated "outsiders" before. After I left the community I was in, after I left many of those beliefs behind, I was just as sure of my beliefs as I had ever been. Convincing others of my right-ness was just as important as ever.

My second step was to change the way I actually held the beliefs. I recognized the limitations to my way of thinking about the universe. Rather than wrapping my fingers so tightly around the beliefs that nobody would ever be able to yank them away, I opened my hand wide.

I used to think that my closest brothers and sisters were the people who matched the content of my beliefs. These were people who called themselves Christians. This important connection was in the content of our beliefs.

When I began to realize that I didn't have to view the crucifixion as God taking Divine anger out on an innocent Son, when I was sure that the concept of lots of people burning forever in hell made no sense, when I landed on new answers to a number of important questions, I thought that this was the important transition. I thought this changing of those beliefs was a deconstruction.

As it turns out, the change in my beliefs was the prologue.

## Deconstructed Beliefs

As I fell deeper into spiritual practice, as my deconstruction continued, I saw that there were some important similarities between certain types of people. They believed they were literally correct. They were profoundly interested in the types of beliefs a person held, less interested in the ways that they might hold these beliefs. Let's call them fundamentalists. I don't think it's inaccurate to say that there are fundamentalist Christians, fundamentalist Buddhists, and fundamentalist agnostics.

There are a lot of ways that the fundamentalist Christian has more in common with the fundamentalist Buddhist than they do with me, despite the fact that both would resist this claim, and despite the fact that both the Christian fundamentalist and I identify with the Christian label.

Similarly, in many ways the deconstructed Muslim has more in common with me than the fundamentalist Christian does. I still follow Jesus. So does the fundamentalist Christian. But the way we do it is so very different. The way we hold our beliefs is so different, even if the beliefs are similar.

If this book could travel backward in time, if I could have read several years ago the words I would eventually write, I would have been quite puzzled by the title of this chapter. I would have assumed the question "How do my beliefs work now?" meant something like, "What beliefs am I supposed to have now?"

These are two very different questions though. "What beliefs am I supposed to have now?" is the question of fundamentalists. They believe that there's only one way to hold a belief. "How do my beliefs work now?" is the question of a deconstructed person.

Let me be clear, here. I don't believe the things we believe are irrelevant. In terms of the scope of this book, however, I am doing my best to leave them aside. Experience has taught me that in the middle of a spiritual transition, the question of what to believe often works itself out. We human beings, it seems, require a little more support in the area of how we ought to hold these beliefs.

Deconstruction is an interesting thing. There are some in religious circles who believe that the next step for them is a reconstruction. I resist this idea. In my experience, these "reconstructed" people are often holding their new beliefs in exactly the same way they were holding their old beliefs.

Some people come to an authentic reconstruction in a low key manner. They might have begun with an understanding that the ways you hold beliefs are important. Or the transition into this realization may not be particularly difficult for them. If you were one of those lucky souls, I suspect you would not be reading a book on this topic.

There is a popular notion that these sorts of reconstructed beliefs are somehow more lukewarm than their fundamentalist counterparts. There is an idea that many fundamentalists would support that a deconstructed Christianity is Christianity-lite.

I, of course, would beg to differ. This is one of those times that my desire to leave space for everyone is at odds with my lived experiences. It seems to me that the people wanting to find literal explanations for all their truth claims are the ones who fail to take their faith seriously. If I told you that the early bird catches the worm, and you set your alarm to wake up at dawn tomorrow to go looking for the early bird and his worm, I could, I think, accuse you of trivializing the statement I made. I suspect that fundamentalists do some of the same trivializing.

I am not sure that deconstructed beliefs are ones for which we can posit a simple and straightforward definition, but there are a few qualities worth noting at this time:

- A deconstructed belief is one that is aware that there are things it doesn't know.

- A deconstructed belief trusts the process.

- A deconstructed faith believes that there are some truths not easily expressed in a simple, word-based manner, and the literal meaning may not be the most important one.

## Deeper Than Words

In short, these new beliefs are our journey to the essence. We always had this intuition that things should have been different, they should have been better. Before our transition, we believed in the possibility of the beliefs themselves. We believed that the words themselves are the most important thing. We believed that this was the final answer. Eventually, though, we learn that there is something deeper than the literal meaning. Something truer than the words. We look for what lies at the heart. We search for an essence deeper than propositions.

Before this realization, before this transition, we were, perhaps, making an idol out of the words. This is the comfort zone of fundamentalists. Western civilization is quite good at this. We describe a thing in terms of the characteristics it has. The coffee is hot and dark. The ice cream is cold and soft. The shovel is metal and four feet long. Knowing is a sort of dissection: we carve and we cut and we analyze.

Much of the talking and thinking about God that we have inherited in the West is the result of this tradition. This tradition, which uses words, images, and symbols to describe God, is called the kataphatic. In kataphatic theology, we generally assume that our words and thoughts are up to the task of describing even God.

The alternative to kataphatic theology is apophatic theology. This theology is built around focusing on the limitations to our thoughts and words. It seeks to empty the mind of all imagery.

Within the Christian tradition, apophatic theology is called the via negativa sometimes, which is associated with the desert fathers and mothers. They were a group who left the comfort and predictability of their lives in the Roman Empire. They grew tired of the increasing interconnections between government and religion. They felt that the Empire was swallowing their beliefs whole. And so they left that world of easy answers behind and went to hermitages in the desert of Egypt. They refused to identify God with any human concept. They insisted that God transcends any thought we can have about who and what the Divine is.

Across traditions, the apophatic is the path of the person who begins to suspect they have grown too comfortable. It is the way of the person who fears their confidence might have become arrogance somewhere along the way.

I love to remind myself about the desert fathers and mothers. Sometimes, my criticism of my former spiritual home feels so uniquely modern. But when I look back, across thousands of years, I can see that there is not much new about my situation. Long before the English language even existed, there was a group who resisted the idea that Jesus subscribes to the dominant political ideology.

The desert mothers and fathers are often credited with developing a technique known as apophatic meditation. Apophatic meditation is a great exploration into the limits of language. Though many forms of meditation help to hone our experience of nondualism, this takes a unique central role in the practice of apophatic meditation.

At its most basic, apophatic meditation is a system of three simple statements:

- An affirmation.

- A negation.

- A negation of a negation.

For example, a cycle of apophatic meditation might begin with focusing on the sentence "God is father" (affirmation). "God is not father" (negation). "God is not not father" (negation of the negation).

The first two statements are fairly straightforward. There are ways that a certain thing is true. There are other ways that thing is not true. I will share a few things about the third statement here, before we give apophatic meditation a try. I will have some more things to say after we give it our first attempt.

There are many ways to express that third statement in writing. For example, we can use print to emphasize the first "not" as in: God is *not* not father. There is a certain wisdom and meaning to expressing it this way. That wisdom and meaning is something like "I am not saying it's accurate when I claim that God is not father," but that statement is simply one approximation of the idea that God is not not father.

On the other hand, placing a hyphen between the nots—as in: God is not-not father—highlights the idea that both "nots" are needed together. They do more than cancel each other out. There is a difference in meaning between the affirmation, "God is father" and "God is not-not father." As can be seen in the value of the slang use of two words placed together for effect. If I said, "I was angry, but not angry-angry." Placing the two words together carries a different shade of meaning.

We could continue with dozens of different combinations of hyphens, italics, and more. Much like a photograph, such precise focus on one tiny detail tends to obscure the clarity of the rest. Rather than continuing to use words to express how imprecise our words and thoughts are, let's try to live in that experience.

# Practice 12
# Apophatic Meditation I

- *Inhale.*

- *Exhale.*

- *Inhale.*

- *Exhale.*

- *Inhale and think or say, "God is within."*

- *Exhale.*

- *Inhale. Think or say, "God is not within."*

- *Exhale.*

- *Inhale. Think or say, "God is not not within."*

- *Exhale.*

- *Inhale.*

- *Exhale.*

- *Inhale.*

- *Exhale.*

- *Inhale. Think or say, "God is outside of me."*
- *Exhale.*
- *Inhale. Think or say, "God is not outside of me."*
- *Exhale.*
- *Inhale. Think or say, "God is not not outside of me."*
- *Exhale.*
- *Inhale.*
- *Exhale.*
- *Inhale.*
- *Exhale.*
- *Inhale. Think or say, "God is love."*
- *Exhale.*
- *Inhale. Think or say, "God is not love."*
- *Exhale.*
- *Inhale. Think or say, "God is not not love."*
- *Exhale.*

- *Inhale.*
- *Exhale.*
- *Inhale. Think or say, "God is real."*
- *Exhale.*
- *Inhale. Think or say, "God is not real."*
- *Exhale*
- *Inhale. Think or say, "God is not not real."*

*If you wish, you could repeat these sentences or try the exercise with some of your own.*

☙☙☙☙☙☙☙☙☙☙☙☙☙☙☙

There are so many powerful statements that can be used in apophatic meditation. The value here is that we learn to hold both a statement and that statement's opposite, and to transcend both of these statements in the negation of the negation.

Like many forms of meditation, the object here is not to release thoughts entirely. My experience of apophatic meditation is that the first time I try out a sentence, I need, in some sense, to prove to myself that each affirmation, negation, and negation of the negation holds up. For example, the first time I work my way through the statement "God is within," I might hold that thought for a while and think, "Okay, yup. I can agree with that."

Then I move to "God is not within." And as I consider that, I realize that this is true too.

Finally, of course, is "God is not not within." One way for my brain to translate this is, "Well, I could not accurately just leave it alone when I said "God is not within," because there is more to the story than just this."

As I repeat that particular group of sentences, it becomes easier to return to use them without doublechecking it. It is as though I have already vetted the three sentences. They check out, I don't need to rethink it every single time. Furthermore, though, as every imaginable sentence ends up working as an affirmation, negation, and negation of a negation, I increase in my faith that that it will almost always work even with a sentence I have never tried before

Eventually, as I repeat this practice with these same phrases, much of my mind becomes more and more restful. Some meditative practices—including this one—are helpful because they occupy just enough of the mind. It is very difficult to truly think about nothing. Meditative practices have to give us something to (not) think about; but there is a sweet spot, between making the mind so busy it is not meditative at all and so subtle that the mind is liable to just start meandering on its own.

One of the reasons apophatic meditation is a valuable practice is because it helps us start to see a new way to think about the things we believe. It sketches an answer to the question, "How are my beliefs even supposed to work now?" Before the ways we carried our beliefs was simple. Straightforward. Dualistic. As we grow, we learn to embrace a full, rich, living complexity. A thing can be this. And also not this. And also not not this.

This is why we sit and meditate. It is not so much about the ten, twenty, or thirty minutes each day we are sitting. It is about taking what we learn into the other twenty-three hours of the day. The obvious thing we take away in a practice like apophatic meditation is the new understanding of the nature of God or wherever else we focused.

But a secondary benefit is that in meditation, we learn what to do when life gets difficult. Do you remember the *Karate Kid* (the good version, from the '80s)? On one level, Daniel was learning to paint the fence. And on one level, we are learning simply to meditate. In a moment of high drama, though, we suddenly see that there was a secret meaning to all the motions Daniel was doing. His painting of the fence was a way for him to learn certain motions he would later use for quite a different purpose. Similarly, if we have worked on saying "God is father" and "God is not father" and "God is not-not father," we just might find something new and exciting happens when we bump into our old "friend" from the spiritual community from which we are deconstructing.

The naive view would be to feel like we have to decide about this person: Are they friend or foe? Are they helpful or hurtful? But practice with many forms of meditation, especially apophatic, makes it easier to do something new and different. When this person approaches us in the aisles of the grocery store, and he says something that seems a masterpiece of passive aggression, we don't stop when we say, perhaps only to ourselves, "That was intentional." In the same breath, and at the same time we realize, "That was not intentional," and we can even continue with, "That was not not intentional." We, like Daniel, are suddenly learning that this practice we had, this thing we did in silent isolation, suddenly has a wider purpose.

Furthermore, as we are wrestling with our feelings about this person, we might think, "He is my friend." But because we have been doing apophatic meditation, we also realize, "He is not my friend" and, of course, "He is not not my friend."

For every one time that we do this specifically and consciously, there might be dozens more that the mere practice leads us to be a little more comfortable with living in the grey area. We might do this subconsciously, or just sit with the reality a little easier that others' words are both harmful and helpful, that they are both friend and not-friend.

I have seen this dynamic at play with other practices, too. At a time when centering prayer was an important part of my practice, I grew quite comfortable releasing intrusive thoughts during my meditation time. But it was in the middle of everyday life with all its hectic intrusiveness that a potentially upsetting reality came crashing into me during a calm dinner one evening. It was fascinating, realizing I could release my desire to control the outcome. It felt very much like simply dismissing an intrusive thought with the word I chose in centering prayer, but it was different. Because this wasn't just a thought: it was a real possibility that would have complicated my life. And I wasn't meditating; it was here and now in the middle of my everyday life. But I had practiced using this tool during centering prayer, and now it waited for me in a mental toolbox where I could readily use it.

This chapter will close with a second example of apophatic meditation. This variation is a little more complex. It's worth laying some groundwork for it.

We can use the breath in a lot of different ways in apophatic meditation. We can do the first phrase with the inhale, the next phrase with the exhale, and the final phrase with the inhale. Or we can create space between the various phrases by only engaging the phrases with each inhale. Or we can create additional spaces between the completed cycles of three phrases. There are a tremendous number of possibilities.

The thing is, because there are only two breath-parts and there are three phrases, many approaches create a sense of being unbalanced. There is an asymmetry when most of the phrases occur with the in-breath or the out-breath. Sometimes, this is not a bad thing. Other times, it is nice to find a way to balance these. One way to provide this balance is to hold the breath during the negation of the negation. This is exemplified in the next practice.

The practice on the next page is an apophatic meditation that explores something other than the Divine. In this case, the focus is on the spiritual transition itself.

# Practice 13
## Apophatic Meditation II

- *Breathe in.*

- *Breathe out.*

- *With your next inhale, think, "This transition is difficult."*

- *With your next exhale, think, "This transition is not difficult."*

- *Inhale.*

- *In the space between the inhale and exhale, think, "This transition is not not difficult."*

- *Exhale.*

- *With your next inhale, think, "The transition is lonely."*

- *With your next exhale, think "The transition is not lonely."*

- *Inhale.*

- *In the space between the inhale and the exhale, think, "This transition is not not lonely."*

- *Exhale.*
- *With your next inhale, think, "This transition will change who I am."*
- *With your next exhale, think, "This transition will not change who I am."*
- *Inhale.*
- *In the space between the inhale and the exhale, think, "This transition will not not change who I am."*
- *With your next inhale, think, "This transition is mine to control."*
- *With your next exhale, think, "This transition is not mine to control."*
- *Inhale.*
- *In the space between the inhale and the exhale, think, "This transition is not not mine to control."*

*Repeat these sentences, or add your own as time permits.*

As we progress, we will notice that the topics of these chapters are not discrete and independent of each other. The ways we hold our beliefs impact everything else because our beliefs are about everything else. The most obvious subject of our beliefs is what we think about God and our faith tradition. But we have beliefs about what it is to be a good person. About whether reading certain types of books is a good idea. About why we should drive on one side of the street and not the other.

That second apophatic meditation was a practice in recognizing that the things we begin to learn about our beliefs can be generalized. We can hold many of our beliefs in a different way than we did before. This will be a powerful experience even if the adjustment to them is not fun.

Many of those beliefs that once defined us might have come out of our holy books. At this time, we might begin to wonder what we should do about that. In the next chapter, we take a closer look.

# CHAPTER SIX

᪅᪅᪅᪅᪅᪅᪅᪅᪅᪅᪅᪅᪅᪅

# And What About My Holy Books?

In a time that history books call the Enlightenment, it was assumed that all the deepest truths could be expressed with words. The gold standard for how to progress was the philosophical argument. We begin with a number of brute facts. We arrange them in a certain way. We assume that the conclusion implied by this arrangement is true forever and in all circumstances.

Immature spiritual communities have created a copycat of philosophical argumentation. They begin with a collection of unrelated scripture verses, arrange them together just so, and declare that these verse-arguments demonstrate that their fundamental beliefs are correct. Submitting to this understanding is generally the price of admission for participating in these communities.

The thing that no one ever tells us is that we pay such a steep price.

Many of us live out of touch with the cost of going along. There are so many benefits to belonging. It's hard to know the answers to these Big Questions, and there can be a sense of gratitude to the new community. Surely, we think, a place with this much kindness and love, a place that has in some important way set me free, surely this place must have this all right.

## Problems with Scripture

Even if the conclusion is not completely false, the process of endorsing such a microscopic process, so focused on the minutia, is unhealthy. Many holy books, certainly the Bible, possess some terrible, terrible statements. If we claim to endorse every little tiny specific thought, we have to back up some pretty horrific claims.

Most traditions have a series of exceptions set up. Some churches still teach that the biblical details about women submitting to men is a principle worth holding on to. But if we get too worried about the Bible's endorsement of slavery, there is lip service explaining why this doesn't mean what it seems to mean. Churches pat themselves on the back around not changing the meaning of the Bible when they endorse an interpretation that paints homosexuality as a sin, while finding a way to gloss over Jesus' quite undeniable criticism of divorce.

The thing is, if we applied these exceptions universally, we would end up with a very different belief system. Almost without fail, the exception we made for divorce or not covering our hair in church could be applied to our favorite hot-button topics.

For a startlingly long time, that may never even cross our mind. We don't admit to ourselves this could even be a possibility.

Living this way feels safe and comfortable. But it is not.

Context, as they say, is key. The big picture is not easy to wrap up in a single sentence. In many ways, it is not even a possibility. One part of making our way through a spiritual transition is finding a place where I can accept that a story is meant to be a story.

I spent years listening to people summarize the meaning of a Bible story. It never even occurred to me to wonder: if these three points (that the minister told me all started with the same letter) were what God wanted me to know, why didn't God ever just express those three points?

This doesn't mean that the stories are only there for entertainment. The process of working out what a story actually means, however, is much messier than many would have us believe. When one person attempts to distill some sort of universal application that is taken as the single monolithic reason for that narrative's presence in a holy book, so much is lost.

My journey through spiritual transition is one where I landed on loving things like scripture differently than I did before. I do not think I love it less. But it changed, like the relationship with our parents changed as we grew up.

That is not the story for everyone, though. Some people on the other side of a spiritual transition find that the books that once had so much value have very little to offer them now. In some cases, they eventually return to those books. In other cases, they do not.

This can seem scary early on. That's an understandable reaction. But there are a few things worth saying to that fear. There are clearly lots of commonalities between this topic and the one we explored last chapter. We continue to explore beliefs, though of course here we look at where these beliefs come from. It continues to be quite understandable that a person in spiritual transition might come into this chapter hoping to be offered some single new way to understand what to do with holy scriptures. The best thing I believe I can do for you is to sketch out a few possibilities and assure you that if this is an area where you are struggling, you will continue to explore these possibilities. You will find much more convincing and specific explanations than the vague sketches that are being offered.

It is natural to have some fear through this time. Facing these thoughts and fears head on is the best way to progress. It positions us to find new guiding principles to support us in our journey. If we are honest about where we are, we can be intentional about making accommodations for this loss. This is why a spiritual practice can be such a powerful thing. There are not many practical steps more effective at getting in touch with where we really are.

One of my favorite things to ask people in their process of deconstruction is, "What do you wish someone had told you sooner?"

One of the answers to this question that comes up frequently is the idea that we have power and control in this process. We have a hand in how it turns out. There are many processes at work here. We have varying levels of control in these processes. Deconstruction can appear from the outside to be like jumping out of a plane when we don't know if our backpack is loaded with a parachute or a picnic blanket. It can seem like submitting ourselves to a terrifying series of laws and rules we are utterly powerless to impact. When we reflect back on our spiritual experiences, many of us would be more likely to endorse an image that is much less terrifying.

It is less scary than it appeared mostly because it is one where we have lots of control. When I think back to the time I knew I no longer belonged to the spiritual place that had been my home, I can liken this to standing on a snowy slope with skis. Far above me is the place where I once thought I was going. It was possible to fight the incline and make a small bit of progress upward. But it didn't seem like this was what I was built for. Eventually, I realized that skiing downward just made so much more sense. Once I made this decision, I could choose whether to take a fast and direct straight downward trip. I could determine if I zigged or zagged. I could aim myself toward the same place that many other skiers were landing, or I could try to come to the level ground far away from all the others.

The point here is that life is almost always about the intersection of what is happening and the question of what we are going to do about those happenings. We have a measure of control over whether things like scripture (and God and prayer and community) continue to play a significant role in our lives.

Continuing to expect that the Bible was some sort of black-and-white rule book would have been like trying to ski uphill. I could have done it through concentrated effort and a decided disinterest into what would have made my soul sing. There was the possibility of wind rushing in my ears, the adrenaline, and the excitement, not to mention the fact that all these tools I had seemed like they were made to assist in going down the hill.

The oversimplified version is that I could accept the words of scripture at face value or I could throw them away. It didn't feel like many other options had ever been extended to me before this. One of the earliest things I learned, however, was that scope matters. Individual phrases are easily weaponized. Oftentimes, when a page or a complete story is looked at, the combined meaning of these words flies in the face of an individual statement. A second early lesson was that I became wary of allowing others to furnish a neatly divided list for me. On one side would be the people from the stories I ought to emulate. These figures are of course the heroes. On the other side of the page are the villains. These are the people I ought to avoid. In some cases, I think now that these lists put the figures on the wrong side of the page. In most cases, the stories are much too rich and nuanced to allow for this kind of dualistic list to make any kind of sense at all. In many cases, all of the figures who appear in the story are both heroes and villains.

Rejecting a hero-and-villain list led to one of the next things I discovered as I began to ski down that slope. This was to look for elements in the story that the people who want to interpret for me don't even want to acknowledge are there.

For example, I remember trying to read the psalms through the lenses that were given to me. There are beautiful psalms about the universal longing for love. There are transcendent psalms where incredibly brave writers bare their heart and soul. There are also many psalms where the speaker gleefully looks forward to God's utter annihilation of the worldly enemy. They look like the musings of a petulant middle schooler who just fell under the protection of the school's biggest bully, except for the writer is wanting more than wedgies for his enemies. He is eagerly looking forward to the babies of his enemies having their brains bashed out on the rocks.

There are still important lessons here. I can read the psalms today as a record of how multi-faceted we humans are. We can long for love and speak in sublime metaphors about our highest aspirations. We can do this even while we are wishing infanticide on our enemies. The psalms teach about how violence begets violence. They teach me about the sorts of damage you can do to a person, that the physical wounds aren't the worst ways we can be broken.

Rather than listening to scriptures as a monologue, I am now in dialogue with them. I wrestle with the nature of the characters, the nature of the stories, and the nature of the books themselves. Is the Bible different from other holy books? Is it different from secular books that have impacted me on so many levels? The first time we admit to ourselves that we are asking these questions is both terrifying and invigorating.

The truth is that my answers don't matter much. They aren't worth sharing here. Asking these questions is more important than the answers. Because the truth is, there's no avoiding wrestling with this sort of meaning. The only thing that is negotiable is whether or not we admit to ourselves that is happening.

## Lectio Divina

A practice called *Lectio Divina*—Latin for "Sacred Reading"—provides for me a welcome antidote to reading with someone else's agenda. Instead of finding the things that some other person wants us to find, the hope with *Lectio* is that we are guided by God.

Even if a person wasn't wanting to recognize the possibility of God, an argument can still be made for the value of this practice. Many of us believe that we possess a wisdom that runs deeper than the things we know and say. The subconscious reaches out with dreams and intuitions. Even if there is no God, *Lectio* gives the subconscious an opportunity to speak directly to us.

There are many ways that this practice has been enacted. What all these different methods have in common is a focus on four stages: read, meditate, pray, contemplate. *Lectio Divina* rose up as a Christian practice, and it is traditionally done with the Bible. Parallel practices have also risen up in other traditions and some are strikingly similar. It can be fruitful to explore other writings using these methods, to try *Lectio* with books that are not the Bible. Other tradition's holy books, poems, even secular books can be used in these practices.

If you have a hope of forging a new relationship with the scripture of the tradition you are leaving, it can be worthwhile to use that book, even if this is a little bit uncomfortable. As always, please practice good self-care and wise discernment. If the process of using that book is too painful, please consider using something else, or for now, skip over this practice.

Whatever you decide to use, reading more than a page is generally not advised. In many cases, you might begin with as little as a paragraph or two. Two major things will help determine the ideal length of a passage for you. Your overall level of comfort with spiritual practices in general and *Lectio* in particular are quite relevant here. As you grow more familiar with this practice, you might be prepared to take on passages of increasing lengths. The second issue focuses on how easy you find the passage to read. If the passage is difficult, or reading is not your preferred method of learning about the world, a smaller selection is most likely advantageous.

## Practice 14
## Lectio Divina

- *Be ready with your reading: have the book or website open and ready for the section you would like to consider.*

- *Spend a few minutes breathing and releasing your worries.*

- *As best you can, with your exhalations, let go of your preconceptions and assumptions of what you are about to read. With each out breath, let go of more of the things you think you know about the reading. Do your best to see these assumptions dissipating into the air.*

- *When you feel you have reached a state of beginner's mind, where all preconceptions have been erased, read the passage all the way through. On this first reading, just try to get a sense about the big picture.*

- *When you finish reading through, give yourself some time to breathe.*

- *Reread the passage. Pay attention to the passages that bring about a reaction in you. Where do you feel stirred?*

- *Read the passage at least one more time. This time, try to find a specific phrase. Ideally, it should not be more than five words long; at most, it should not be more than ten words long. If you get to the end of the passage and have not found anything, that is okay. Read the passage—or at least a portion of the passage—one last time to select a few sacred words that speak to you.*

- *Say your words out loud. You might wish to assign one half of the phrase to your inhale, and one half of the phrase to your exhale.*

- *Spend a good portion of the time repeating your sacred phrase from your reading. Leave yourself access to the source material, so you can remind yourself of the wording if you get off track.*

- *When you are ready, release your sacred words. Sit in wordless union.*

# Arguing and Holy Books

When we are deep within the story of one specific faith community, it is natural to see that community's perspective as one that is the most convincing. Often, the holy scriptures of that community are used to prop up these beliefs. If the power structure has declared that the meaning of this thing is X, there is not much reason to go investigating this. It is natural to accept this at face value.

So when we are in that frame of mind, we don't find ourselves very interested in context. We accept the verses without considering the paragraph, chapter, or book. We accept the interpretation of this person who is within the group, because their group membership trumps the credentials, opinion, or experience of the person who is outside the group.

And of course, we do this for so much more than just Bible verses. This failure to consider context comes into laser-sharp focus when we look at the ways spiritual traditions treat their holy books. But once we are on the lookout, we see this failure to consider context in so many other places.

Sometimes, as we leave that community behind, our new understanding of these topics comes from the simple fact that we are not so interested in building a simple argument constructed of naked facts that have been stripped out of their context.

For example, there is a wide, loud, and passionate debate about the nature of racism. There are some who identify a small selection of facts they consider all important. These facts are piled up nicely to construct the following argument:

1.  Racism is a result of people intentionally thinking their ethnic group is better than other ethnic groups.

2.  Everyone I know truly believes that their ethnic group is no better than anyone else's. Therefore, racism is no longer a major problem.

These arguments are often propped up by out-of-context quotations from scriptures. I have often heard the argument above justified with the promise that "in Christ there is no Jew or Gentile, no slave or free person, there is no man or woman." (It is worth noting that many of these houses of worship suddenly find an interest in context when questioned on why they can continue to treat men and women differently if they are all one in Christ.)

An understanding of racism that is more contextual is less interested in what is intended. This understanding looks at the differences between ethnic groups in areas like income, education, incarceration. It ends up being more difficult to express with sound bites. When it is not finessed into a conveniently formulated philosophical argument, it is less likely to emphatically endorse a single course of action as the absolute cure-all for the entire problem.

It is difficult, sometimes, to know how to best interface with these arguments. Even when I can get past the projection others have toward me—and even when I get past the projection I have toward others—when someone attempts to engage in a carefully constructed argument that is rooted in a myopic view of a few out-of-context Bible verses, I have a desire to fire back with a few out-of-context Bible verses of my own.

I am increasingly convinced this is unwise for two interdependent reasons. First, when I engage someone in a Battle of the Out-of-Context Verses, I am demonstrating my belief that ultimately these disagreements can be settled by resorting to that microscopic level. Thus I am communicating the idea that this is a valid way to use the Bible. Second, when I argue with others about the nature of Truth, I am demonstrating that I believe arguments are likely to settle things. Even if I refrain from relying on individual verses, when I construct arguments to counter someone else's arguments, I am acting as though I believe at the end of the day we can look at all of this out-of-context logic and make a rational decision. I just don't see much evidence that bears out this idea. What I see in my life is that people go through a process. This process engages their heart and mind. It embraces logic and emotion. It includes the individual and the collective. It doesn't happen in a debate context.

Even reading itself can become a process that relies primarily on rationality. Rather than accepting a story for what the story is and does, we apply our rationality to it and seek to distill out a series of principles. Billy Collins laments this approach to poetry in his wonderful Introduction to Poetry where he offers up some wise and whimsical ways that we might fully engage the text on its own terms. He laments that what "they" (students, perhaps) want to do is tie the poem to a chair and beat it with a hose to find out what it means. This can be done with prose, too. Many religious communities have been tying their texts to a chair and beating it with a hose as if it were a reluctant witness in a film noir. This approach is the rational one, looking for principles and rules that we can infer and apply universally. It is, fortunately, not the only way to read a text.

There is a practice sometimes quite closely allied to *Lectio Divina*. This practice, which I will call "Holy Imagining," is associated with St. Ignatius. It asks us to bring our senses to the passages we read. It is most directly applicable to passages with a strong narrative sense, asking us to place ourselves, in the imagination, into the narrative that is unfolding. We choose a character, and let the scene unroll in our mind. This character could be a major figure. It might be an unnamed member of a crowd. It could be anyone—or any animal—present in the scene.

It is easy to go the way of an over-reliance on out-of-context rationality and turn this into a fact-finding mission. The temptation is to want to turn this into a research project and live in the scene as it actually appeared. That is an adventure in missing the point! The idea with holy imagining is to first embrace the possibility that the event could have occurred, and then to accept the story on the story's own terms, to live in the senses and from the perspective of one of the participants of this narrative.

# Practice 15
## Holy Imagining

- *Read through one to two pages of narrative.*

- *Read again, this time searching for a passage between a quarter and three-quarters of a page that particularly speaks to you.*

- *Read the passage, identifying the characters that are either explicitly mentioned or implied. Explore who you might be in this scene.*

- *Imagine (perhaps by rereading) the scene from this character's perspective.*

- *Consider all the senses: How does it sound there? How does it look? How does it smell? What is the temperature? Can you reach out and touch anything there?*

- *Can you imagine any additions to the scene not expressed by the text—*

*perhaps what happens immediately before or after?*

- *Reread the whole selection.*

- *Spend some time exploring why this perspective came to you and what you learned through the experience.*

Make no mistake. Engaging in *Lectio Divina* and Holy Imagining will help you begin to think of your holy book in a new way. This process is a good thing. But it won't always be easy, especially as it pertains to relationships with other people from the tradition you are leaving.

It can be frustrating and difficult to let others have their say when it comes to their beliefs about scripture. It takes patience to reach a place where I resist the urge to respond. (By the way, sometimes, I don't resist the urge to respond.) On some occasions, something or someone needs to be defended. Sometimes, that something is my own sense of self. That is no small thing. There are times it is worthy to defend my integrity and autonomy. But most of the time? Most of the time, it would have been better for everyone, including me, if I had let the other person have their say.

I don't need to shrug my shoulders. I don't need to pretend to agree. I also have the right to choose whom I engage and when I engage. There is a very, very small list of people who have a right to expect that I owe them an explanation for the things I do, the things I say, and the things I think. Unfortunately, there is a very long list of people who believe they have a right to expect that I owe them an explanation for the things I do, the things I say, the things I think. Their beliefs, however, do not have to be my reality.

There are a few things that can help these situations, when someone wants to force a confrontation. One of the best things I have ever been taught, in my work with emotionally challenged youth, is the power of lowering my voice. When someone approaches me with aggression, such as a raised voice, intense body language, or any of the rest, the most powerful thing I can do is to choose to be quieter than them. This does not have to be an act of meekness. This can be an act demonstrating that I am in control when the other person is not.

A robust spiritual practice will make these confrontations much more tolerable. Some unhealthy communities have eroded our belief in ourselves and our right to formulate boundaries. Regular meditation can bring some healing in these areas.

Anxiety about the end result of confrontations can lead to unrealistic fears about what might happen when we face someone. Contemplative activities can also lower anxiety because they encourage us to face our fears rather than continue to run from them.

Often we are not very good at assessing the size of the things in our minds. The things we think are going to be enormous sometimes turn out to be much less than we expected. And the things we expected to be small may be huge.

An exploration of our changing relationship to holy scripture, for example, would seem like it is quite straightforward. But it quickly becomes clear that there are other things involved in this, things like our overarching relationship with the truth, and our relationship with other people who suddenly have a different view of the Bible than we used to. As these friends watch my relationship with the Bible evolve, they would probably think that the Bible is becoming less important to me. Indeed, these well-intentioned people would tell anyone who listens that their entire faith is in the Bible alone. I suspect that they even believe it.

Let's wander down that rabbit hole just a bit.

We come back, yet again, to the belief that a series of facts without context are sufficient. The most immediate problem of course, is the difficulty in answering the question, "Why? Why did you base your faith on the Bible?"

The answer to this question, generally speaking, is, "Because the Bible told me to."

One of the difficulties with this answer is that many holy books tell adherents that they should place faith in them. If we privilege the Bible above these other books, then we must have some reason to listen when the Bible tells us to, and to shut out the Koran when it makes equal claims. Since it is clear that this reason can't be internal to the Bible, it must be outside the Bible. Since it is outside the Bible, it is difficult to see how that person could claim that all their beliefs are based on the Bible.

Even if somebody could sidestep the preceding dilemma, they would be faced with a second one. This problem is this: the Bible does not interpret itself. Centuries of infighting, thousands of denominations, countless battles over theology after theology make it abundantly clear that there is no easy, monolithic understanding. At the end of the day, perhaps some of these ideas will be shown to be right, while others will be shown to be wrong. But this demonstration is rooted in things outside the Bible. Furthermore, the Bible was not written as a single, coherent document; instead, it was written by many authors over the course of more than a thousand years. When it references scripture in the Christian portions of the Bible (the "New Testament"), it is referring to the Hebrew scriptures (the "Old Testament"), since the New Testament did not yet exist.

# Other Roots

There are several things in which my beliefs are rooted. The Bible is one of them. It is not the only one. There is no alternative to this situation. It is this way even for people who insist that the Bible is the only foundation for their beliefs. The only choice we have in the matter is whether we are honest with ourselves and the people around us.

Some of the more common things that provide the other foundations for faith include tradition, personal experience, logic, and Nature. It is not that I have dialed down the importance of the Bible. It is that I have turned up my awareness of the importance of those other things. An entire book could (and should!) be written on each of these topics.

There are surely some potential foundations I am missing, and I'm sure I use some you will find unnecessary. Regardless of what each individual relies on, in a healthy belief system more than one factor is at work as a foundation. Often the conclusion of one enhances the other. Sometimes, the conclusion of one exists in a tension with the other. There are times when I can work this tension out. There are other times that I have to sit in the discomfort of this tension, accepting it as a part of the way of the world.

It ought to be noted that one of the things we are doing as we engage in spiritual practices is reclaiming the traditions of our spiritual ancestors. We are participating in activities that have helped grow peace and strength across the centuries. These practices also bring us a treasure chest full of personal experiences, and the faith in our own self to trust these experiences as rooted in reality.

Lots of spiritual practices are built around a love of Nature. We will close this chapter with one of them. This practice will require access to some aspect of Nature. Ideally, this would be a hiking trail. If need be, it could be a walk along a city street or even a few minutes in a small yard.

# Practice 16
# Nature Adoration

- *Find a calm place with lots of Nature present.*

- *Begin a slow, meandering walk. Be present and aware of your surroundings. Keeping an air of calm, do your best to discover something new in this place.*

- *Be on the lookout for a particular object that speaks to you. Perhaps it is a cloud, a rock, or the way the shadows of a leaf lands on the grass. It needn't be big or beautiful in any classic kind of sense. You might know this thing right away when you see it. You might walk past, consider it for a while, and return.*

- *When you have chosen the thing you will adore, open yourself to it.*

- *Study it with love, as if you had to memorize it. Describe its appearance.*

- *Apply your other senses to it: listen to it, smell it and touch it, if possible.*

- *If you are comfortable with this idea, experience this object as the unfolding of God.*

- *When you are done with your time of adoration, let this object go. Consider whether you have a new understanding. Ask yourself whether you could put this understanding into words.*

- *If you wish, keep this object in your mind as an icon of God's presence in the world.*

# CHAPTER SEVEN

֍֍֍֍֍֍֍֍֍֍֍֍֍֍֍֍

# Can I Fully Embrace Nondualism?

My best guess is that this chapter is going to be either your favorite chapter or your least favorite. We're going to take a little walk into some pretty weird spaces for a bit. Will you bear with me? I promise the next chapter will be the most grounded of all the chapters so far. So if this stuff is hard for you, hang in there. Things will soon take a turn in quite a different direction.

The challenge here is not only how abstract this topic is. Taking a deeper dive into nondualism is difficult because by its very nature it runs deeper than words. This topic is also challenging here because in the writing of this book I am walking a fine line. There is a balance I am trying to get right.

On the one hand, I am trying to blaze a wide path that leaves room for lots of different types of experiences. We have lots of things in common as we go through a spiritual transition. We are looking for the very essence of the religion we once participated in. In many important ways, it is the same essence that we are all looking for.

Yet there will be differences. There will be differences that are unavoidable in terms of where we are coming from. Perhaps, more important, there will be good and useful differences in terms of where we are headed. My goal for this book is to walk with you through a process, so I don't wish to prescribe a specific destination.

To be more specific: my own destination turned out to be mysticism—but not everyone comes out of deconstruction declaring themselves a mystic. I believe that everyone who deconstructs will have a renewed sympathy for what a mystic is up to. But they might find themselves on a different path. However, the topic of this chapter is most relevant to the readers who find themselves mystics.

One of the most important things I can offer to anyone in a time of spiritual transition is to urge a slowness about this process. Sit with all the possibilities. Recognize your power in this process. You get to choose how this goes.

In six months or a year or two years, some aspects of this deeper dive into nondualism may not be as relevant to you—or it may be more relevant. I am thinking as I write this about my kid's tour of a technical high school. Representatives of each of the school's shops had gathered at an introductory fair, each displaying some sort of artifact that their shop made. There were robots, car engines, wood structures. The biotechnology shop even displayed petri dishes with the organism they had cloned. The incoming freshman would not have been able to make those things. That was the whole point, in a way: to showcase some of the fruits of the journey of a particular path.

If this chapter is a struggle, think of it like some project shared from a potential path. A proof of what that particular end-game has to offer. On that preview day, the items being showcased had to have some sort of interest to the average person. If the item required tons of technical skill but was so obscure in its purpose that potential students couldn't see its value, there would have been little point. Nondualism is a good choice on this front. Even non-mystics will find themselves

dabbling in it during times of spiritual deconstruction. The benefits are quite apparent.

So let's begin.

# Fundamentalism

Many of us find ourselves, spiritually speaking,
beginning in a place of fundamentalism. I am
using that word in a funny way here, stretching
the limits of its definition. Defined in a narrow,
traditional way, fundamentalism can be said to
apply to a relatively narrow group of religious
people. These fundamentalists may live in the
American South. They are no fans of Darwinian
evolution. They might be conservative Baptists
occupying churches with uncomfortable pews and
singing hymns.

None of these specifics are the things that I
am thinking about when I use the term here. By
fundamentalist, I mean a person who has a certain relationship with the laws and expectations
of their chosen spiritual home. There is a liter-
alism here. A black-and-white view of the world.
A hostility to other ways of looking at things. A
hesitation around being charitable to other views.

Under this broader view of the term, fundamentalism is not limited to Christianity or even
religions. An atheist might be a fundamentalist.

A capitalist or a communist might be a fundamentalist. A Republican or a Democrat might be
a fundamentalist. I think it is easier to recognize this in the ideology that we do not endorse.
"People like me aren't that rigid," we might be
tempted to think. I am sympathetic to that view.
But I cannot endorse this idea, as tempting as I
might find it. Perhaps the actual numbers vary.
Maybe there are more fundamentalists within a
certain area or group. But there are some fundamentalists everywhere. This is true because
fundamentalism is such a natural place to begin.
The words mean what we expect them to mean.
Literal truth is the most obvious kind of truth.

Oftentimes we tell ourselves that we are
making progress toward some sort of essence
when in fact we are simply trading one fundamentalism for another. Many people talk about
deconstructing out of this group and now quite
militantly ally themselves with that group. It is
not that this step is unimportant. But it is not a
movement in the direction we might think it is. It
ends up being a parallel step, no further and no
closer to the essence than when we began.

Yet it is important. For many of us, the first
ideology that we land in is the most difficult to
leave. We haven't figured out how to let go of our
beliefs. Switching up one fundamentalism for

another is an important step in terms of learning that we actually can choose whether we are a Baptist or a Lutheran, a Christian or a Buddhist, a capitalist or a communist, a Republican or a Democrat.

It seems that this is an important step for so many of us because switching up which specific fundamentalism we endorse gives us the opportunity to discover that none of them satisfy. This is where we begin to intuit that perhaps we are changing the wrong sorts of things. Perhaps it is not the ideas we need to switch so much as the manner in which we are holding them.

## Nuances

Early in the journey, it seems like we have only two choices: we can be religious or not. This is one of the problems with dualistic thinking. It conflates all the nuanced possibilities we might have chosen between. Often, the oversimplifications we have created leave us with two possibilities, both of which are rather unpleasant.

We take a second step as we begin to understand that there are more than these two choices. In the case of spirituality, we begin to see that one important question is about what we believe. We might identify this by stating that we are a

Muslim or a Jew, a Christian or a Rastafarian. The second important question is about how we believe it. Here we might choose a descriptor like fundamentalist or mystic, progressive or traditional. This second transition becomes less about the content of our beliefs and more about our relationship to these ideas. Even as these are important steps in nondualism, it is still, however, only part way there.

Defining and talking about dualism is tricky. If we see dualism/nondualism as a pair of options to choose between, suddenly we are back in the realm of duality. Nondualism is necessarily something that begins to transport us beyond the ability of words to convey. Words themselves can trap us in dualisms when we take them too seriously. The recognition that words will fail us is no small thing when it comes to thinking about our everyday, mundane experiences. As we begin to grapple with ideas, forces, and beings that are by definition transcendent, it becomes even more important.

Let's try on an example. Think about the best day you have had in recent memory: the sights, the smells, the feelings, the tastes and the sounds. If you told me about that day, would I fully understand it? I believe that the answer to that question is a resounding "no." And if our words would fail to convey all that there is to be known about this day, how could they possibly ever describe Buddha or Atman or God?

Let me try one other way of getting at this, by borrowing an image from Zen Buddhism. A man pointed at the moon. His companion kept staring at his finger. Our words are like the finger. When we get stuck there, we are missing something vital.

The Christian community I left would pay lip service to the idea that Christ is within us one week. The next week there would be a little of attention paid to the idea that we are within Christ. They would throw both of these phrases around. But I never saw anybody try to hold them both together at the same time. I wonder what would happen if we really did try to take these images together. Can we do it? Picture them both at the same time?

Yes. And also no. Nondualism is the domain of the mystics.

When I try to hold these images together, there are some things that arise. Thoughts about who I am and who God is, and where we connect. Really sitting with these conflicting images is helpful for me. It gives a picture in my mind that I could have never held by considering these ideas one at a time. Dualism tells us that X can be inside of Y: my milk carton can be inside of that paper bag over there. Or Y can be inside of X: we could crumple up the paper bag and leave it inside the milk carton. Nondualism says maybe the same bag can both be inside of the milk carton and outside of it at the same time.

The fundamentalist community I left would recognize that there is something wonderful in the image that God breathed into the earth and made the first human. But it seems that, according to them, God will never get that breath back. Humanity is forever a separate being from God. My religious background also had quite elaborate and sometimes specific pictures about what happens after this life. The thing worth noticing is that there was an assumption that we would always be different and separate from God.

The more I engage in spiritual practice, the less I can believe this. I grow increasingly convinced that the divide between me and God is both temporary and arbitrary. Someday, I will return to complete union with God.

It is not just me and God, of course. It is me and you. And you and the person whom you have to work so hard to love. We will come to be one. I suspect that this is one of the reasons that forgiveness is so important on the spiritual path. Forgiveness lays the groundwork for reunion in some profound way.

As a Christian mystic, I have dual citizenship in two different countries. One is the "country" of Christianity. The other is the "country" of mysticism. As a Christian, I believe certain things about the nature of Jesus of Nazareth and about God, who made the universe. As a mystic, I have experienced certain things that lead me to believe that the boundaries between all things are permeable. This includes the boundaries between myself and God and the boundaries between the different religious traditions.

This dual citizenship is not a comfortable thing at first. Our old fundamentalism would tell us that this second country is no good. It has to because it is operating in that dualistic mindset of choosing either/or. We can be a Christian. Or we can be a mystic. How could we ever be both?

That seems like a powerful question. No words come up to answer it. Nondualism is not the sort of thing that can be ever ultimately expressed in words. This is taken as a confirmation by fundamentalism. It's all fuzzy thinking and nonsense, all that nondualism. Right?

Maybe. But then again, so is love. Are you planning on giving up on love, fundamentalist? Sometimes, the de facto answer is yes. That is not a road I would like to walk down. Would you?

# The Breath Can Teach Us

Perhaps the most fundamental assumption in the universe is "I am me, and I am separate from the universe and God." An implication of this idea is the conviction that we always will be.

And there is nothing more basic to us than the breath itself. A set of beliefs focused on something as elementary as our breath seems unassailable: there is a me; this me can choose to change my breathing; when it does, my breathing changes. When I decide to slow my breathing down, it slows down. There must be a "me" that is doing the deciding.

But . . . what if there wasn't a me?

Or what if there is a me, but that me doesn't actually do the breathing?

The first time I heard somebody share these possibilities, I thought they were an idiot. So if this is your first thought, I would like to think you are in good company. But then I was faced with a series of considerations about these beliefs. And as I weighed them, I realized that maybe things were not quite as cut and dried as they first appeared.

The first consideration is this: I can't actually explain how I change my breath. I can tell you that sometimes I think about speeding my breath up. At approximately the same time my breath changes. But if there was someone who couldn't change their breath, and they asked me for advice about how to do it, I couldn't actually give them much insight into what to do. There are a few things that are similar to this aspect of breathing. The common view of moving our body around is similar. I think about moving my arm, and it moves. But how am I doing it? Who knows? Not me.

The second consideration is this: my breathing continues to happen when I don't think about it. For some brief periods a day, "I" seem to take control. But for much of my waking time and all of my sleeping time, my breath just seems to happen. This automatic pilot generally does a pretty good job with it. When I am needing more oxygen due to physical demands on my body, it brings in that oxygen by increasing the rate of breathing or through increasing how deeply I breathe.

The third consideration is that psychology, neuroscience, and philosophy are converging in a rare point of agreement about some highly relevant facts here. All three of these fields have recently shown, in their various ways, that we humans love to project narratives and characters where these things simply don't exist. It seems likely that if there was not a "me" to be responsible for things like breathing, we would certainly invent one.

As we start to wrestle with these thoughts, it is easy to focus—even fixate—on the things we are about to lose. Am I nobody, then, without my soul? Am I nothing, if there is no me?

Well, in a way.

But also? You are God.

I was taught, "Here are the humans. There is God." This is called theism. It is the primal dualism, the ultimate either/or. In those spaces where theism reigns, to question this primal assumption is the ultimate act of arrogance. This charge— of arrogance—was quite a powerful weapon. There is something about being accused of being too big for our britches that is quite effective at silencing us.

But one place I can experience nondualism in the breath. This chapter's spiritual practice is a profound way to get at this. You might see familiar elements from early practices here. I found that working at embracing this reality did not so much open a bunch of new spiritual practices as it provided a new dimension to reinvestigate some spiritual practices I had been doing for a while.

## Practice 17
## Oneness

- *Find a relaxed position. Generally speaking, this will be a seated position with feet flat on the floor and spine as straight as is comfortable.*

- *Notice your breath. Allow yourself to be aware of it without seeking to change it.*

- *Feel the inhale: notice where the breath comes in on the nostrils or mouth. Observe the flow of air down the throat and into the belly.*

- *Feel the exhale. Notice the difference in the temperature and moisture of the air as it leaves the body.*

- *Continue this for at least three more breaths. Continue longer if that feels right.*

- *As you continue to observe this process, recall that a story goes that God reached down and breathed into a*

*handful of earth. After that breath,
there was Adam.*

- *Observe the exhale.*

- *Continue this for two more breaths:
  God-in-the-universe is breathing you.*

- *Open your heart and mind to the
  awareness that other people and
  animals in your area (perhaps your
  family in other bedrooms, or the other
  occupants of the building you are in)
  are breathing, too; God-in-the-universe
  is breathing them.*

- *As you complete a second and third
  breath with this awareness, continue
  to observe this breath being breathed
  in you.*

- *Open your mind and heart to the
  plants and even microscopic organisms
  all around you. Some living things
  inhale oxygen and exhale carbon
  dioxide. Others do the reverse. See the
  world breathing in all these creatures.*

- *Sit in this flow and connection for as
  long as you would like.*

- *Can you widen this network of connections? Can you make it geographically larger? Can you expand the nature of the interconnections?*

- *When you are ready, return to your everyday world. Hold on to the connections between the rest of the world that were deepened here.*

## Nondualism as an Escape

Nondualism is very abstract. Thinking about it can sometimes be a challenge, even a distraction. It is important, to be sure. But we can lose sight of some of the immediate and concrete realities if we are not careful. If you are anything like me, when things get difficult or painful, you welcome something that shifts the focus out of the heart and into the head. Even here, there is a dualistic reduction. We don't need to choose between abstraction and concrete reality. We don't need to live either out of the heart or our head. Both are important.

The temptation is to launch ourselves on a quest to understand the nature of nondualism so that we can live out of touch with the painful things that are happening. First, we embark on an intellectual journey into the nature of nondualism. Once we understand it a bit, we take a deep dive into it so that we can escape the anxiety and pain of not knowing where we're at spiritually. This desire is understandable. During a spiritual transition, it makes sense to feel sad. A deconstruction can be a crisis.

But we rob ourselves of opportunities if we venture too far away from these lived realities. One of the opportunities here is to come to terms with the reality that painful things are just painful things. Hurt cannot destroy us. If we never learned this, or need a deep reminder, we can and will carry this lesson with us long after this liminal space is a distant memory.

Not all the challenges you face will be like this one, of course. But I can promise you that there will be challenges ahead. And if we can go through this one in a powerful way, we get to carry the gifts of this challenge on into the next.

# CHAPTER EIGHT

‧𝕯‧𝕯‧𝕯‧𝕯‧𝕯‧𝕯‧𝕯‧𝕯‧𝕯‧𝕯‧𝕯‧𝕯‧𝕯‧𝕯‧𝕯

# Interlude

In the early stages of this transitional process, it is very difficult to establish a regular spiritual practice. Though it is beneficial, it is not easy. This book has now introduced seventeen spiritual practices. Perhaps you know some other ones as well.

It is worth returning to the topic, now, of just what you ought to do with these. It would be almost impossible to incorporate each and every one into a regular spiritual practice. The most straightforward reason for this is simply that there are too many.

With every kind of skill, we have to decide how much we are going to specialize. There are some people who focus on only one thing. There are others who focus on a few different things. It's not many people who are able to split their attention between seventeen different things.

As this book progresses, even more spiritual practices will be introduced. In the first portion of this book, I have had an approach of "let's just throw everything at the wall and see what sticks." As we move to the middle stage of this book—and out of the most scary aspects of transition, hopefully—let's refine this process a little bit.

It's possible you are a fastidious person and you have been carefully building a spiritual practice since the first page of this book. If that is true, you are in great shape. You won't need these next few paragraphs much.

If you have been simply trying each practice, though, and then leaving it behind as we approach the next one, these pages are for you. That was a fine thing to do for where we were. Carpenters need tools before they can build anything. Now you have seventeen tools.

This might be a good time to pause. Review the seventeen practices. Maybe redo a few of them. Remind yourself of what they felt like and how they benefited you. For that reason, this will be one of the few chapters in this book that does not offer a spiritual practice. In place of something new, I'd like to encourage you to return to one (or more) of the practices from prior chapters.

If you have not yet begun to practice any of these every single day, I am going to invite you to do so now. I would challenge you to choose no more than three to practice on a regular basis. It might be that about 30 minutes a day is a good goal for you. When I am able to do two sessions of thirty minutes a day, I feel deep benefits. But even five minutes once a day is much, much better than nothing.

In the upcoming pages, as new practices are introduced, try them out. Consider whether these are worth incorporating into your practice. If you decide that they are, then determine if you will shorten each of the practices or if you will cut something out.

This is one of those cases where less is more. Erring on the side of simplicity is wise. It would be better to rotate through too few practices than too many. This is because we can hide from ourselves and our pain by introducing too much novelty. This can be a constant temptation. I hope you will be on your guard for that.

As time goes by, you might find that the treatment of a practice here was too superficial. You might make the decision to take a deeper dive into something that works well for you. There are lots of wonderful resources available if you would like to learn more about a specific type of contemplative practice. Maybe you will even decide that all of these spiritual practices served you well through your spiritual transition, but now that you are on the other side of it, you can release them. That's always a possibility. But for me? It's well worth the continued investment.

In a few chapters we will face head on the importance of returning to where we began, the importance of viewing much of the journey as a process, not a product. But as we consider the importance of returning back to those earlier spiritual practices, it's worth previewing some of those ideas now.

The first is that this is a symbolic and instructive thing we are doing, circling back to try those older practices again. Many of us are brought up in an environment where "having" to go back has a negative association. In my home of America, we have put much faith in an upward trajectory. This has infected so much, including our spiritual lives.

It is likely that you are transitioning out of a spiritual community that viewed the journey in a straight line. The theory was that you began in a certain space: a certain level of maturity, a certain level of ability, carrying a certain level of concerns. By learning a series of lessons, through a series of pre-arranged classes, you progressed directly away from that starting point and ended up somewhere new.

This view was illustrated by the idea that we are born on Earth, we want to travel "up" to heaven, and we have failed if we went in the opposite direction, "down" to hell. According to this way of thinking, we will stay in that place— either directly above or directly below where we began—forever. Even if a person continues to believe in the truth of the Bible (as your friendly author does), this is an example of very selective reading. There are lots of alternative understandings out there. But the passages that suggest that we are not headed in a straight line away from where we are now are not consistent with the message our culture sends us, so it is easy to filter them out.

The point here is that circling back to the practices early in the book is not a mark of failure. Mature spiritualities speak of the way of descent. Hundreds of books have been written about spiral dynamics. This of course, might lead us to wonder, "Am I meant to go downward? Or in continual circles?"

Actually, it's even more complicated than that. Our society's view that progress can and should occur in a straight line is overdone. But it is not wrong. There are places and times that we should never return to again. Wallowing in pain unnecessarily does not help anybody. Sometimes, progress is up.

Welcome, friends, to another opportunity to practice radical nondualism. Am I meant to descend? Travel in circles? Take a straight line up?

Yes.

# CHAPTER NINE

*ᕫ·ᕫ·ᕫ·ᕫ·ᕫ·ᕫ·ᕫ·ᕫ·ᕫ·ᕫ·ᕫ·ᕫ·ᕫ·ᕫ·ᕫ*

# What Am I Going to Do with My Body?

There are few places, outside of a college class, that anyone is likely to admit to having a "theory of the body." And yet spiritual communities in particular do. A theory of the body is a set of ideas about how the body is important and how it is not. It is a set of beliefs about what we should do with the body and what we should not. This theory plays itself out in so many different arenas. A theory of the body relates to health, wellness, sexuality, fitness, and nutrition. It expresses ideas about physical and emotional illnesses, aging, disability, equity, and fairness.

My departure from the evangelical church began when the mental health of one of my family members began to slip. This struggle had a huge impact on my family. The church, at first, was supportive. Over the long term, though, I received an unspoken message from the people around me. The message was that those experiencing unpleasant events must somehow be to blame. There were lots of people praying for me. There weren't many people crying with me, though. And that is what I needed. I needed them physically with me—bodily with me. It would have not been enough if somebody said they were going to be with me in spirit. A theory of the body has things to say about the brain, and how it interacts with the mind. This is why a theory of the body has something to say about mental health.

As if these areas are all not big enough, a theory of the body includes a lot more. A theory of body includes questions about whose bodies are attractive and what we should do with those deemed attractive and unattractive. In many cases, it might seem that a theory of the body simply wants to ban all sorts of attraction and tell people that they should not act on these feelings. In practice, it's a good deal more complicated than this

Around the time I left that evangelical church, it was being absorbed by a larger, multicampus operation. A dear friend (who was a little bit bigger than society tells women to be) had sung for the church for years. She had the strongest voice on the worship team, and yet she was told that she would have to audition to keep the role she had already been doing, while the other musicians from the old band were allowed to slide right into comparable positions in the new church. Those that were handed a position in the worship band conformed to society's rather arbitrary beauty standards in a way that my friend did not. This too was about a theory of the body.

Questions about what we should do with love, sex, and attraction are explained by what a person believes about the body. Therefore the question of how a church will treat people who are gay, queer, and trans will be determined here. Even the question of social justice largely hinges on these beliefs. If a church devalues physical bodies, it can have a much easier time turning a blind eye when violence is done to bodies. Questions of sexual abuse, slavery, and war will all be colored by how important the physicality is of those who have been hurt.

To the best of my knowledge, no one ever discussed these things. There was no official teaching. It would have been easier if they had. Then we could discuss it, debate it, and perhaps even reach some agreement about what is right and wrong to believe. Though there might have been some sort of doctrine statement about homosexuality, there was certainly no awareness of how interconnected so many apparently diverse issues are. In many cases, these were the places I was the most disappointed with the church. If it had a more healthy view of the body, so much would have been better.

I don't think anyone even knew they were shunning my family. I don't think (though I am not sure) that my friend's exclusion from singing at the church service was a conscious plan. There are people who see this as an excuse. They consider it better that no one did it on purpose. I understand why a person might think this. But it's wrong. This inability to name and own and talk about it is so much worse. It makes it diabolical. So hard to root out.

There is so much good about the body. There is so much worth celebrating. The body has wisdom, and it is a seat of much joy.

The disdain for the physical plays out in interesting ways. There are people who believe that when they die they will leave their bodies and the Earth behind. Lots of very smart people have made very convincing cases that this is not the worldview of the Christian Bible. But to suggest the idea of an embodied afterlife to many Christians is to risk the worst kind of ire from them.

The attitude toward the body is mirrored by the attitude to the Earth. The same people seeking to leave the Earth and the body behind are the types least concerned with catastrophes like climate change and other forms of environmental degradation. How a person feels about the body is likely to reflect how they feel about the whole of the physical world.

It seems like more "sins of the flesh" come out of the church than anywhere else. We might think that the institution that comes down so vocally against expressions of sexuality would be the place that had the fewest issues. Yet it doesn't seem to work that way at all. It seems that even though the church claims to have the most restrictive expectations with sexuality, it also has the most problems.

When viewed in the context of the shadow-self and repression, this is not very surprising. Unrealistic expectations were placed on a community. They tried to talk themselves into being "holy" and "pure." As very human feelings and thoughts emerged, the only thing to do with these "unacceptable" desires was to convince themselves that these unacceptable things were going on outside in the world. And so they focused on the sexuality of others, preached fire-and-brimstone sermons, acted so sure that they had everything just exactly correct. Eventually, they could not project all of the desires they were trying to deny. Eventually they acted. And here we are.

Even when a repressed person does not inflict their misery on the outside world, one of the most depressing repercussions of all this projection about sexuality is that it comes to appear that the body and sex are identical. A person denying their sexuality is denying their embodiment and missing out on so much more. There is so much more to the body than sex. So it is that when many of us transition out of certain spiritual communities, we must reclaim the body in general and our attitudes about sex particularly. This is not an easy thing to do. But it is time and effort well spent.

Looked at from a slightly different perspective, we come back to the so-called Enlightenment. The Enlightenment loved out-of-context arguments. The idolization of logic is a lifting up of the brain, of thought. It is a denigrating of the rest of body, almost inherently. Context is not that different from being embodied. Just as this body is the place and time my soul and mind are located in the world, the specific context and experiences of an event are the place where it is located in the world.

## Practices with the Body

There is a popular notion that many spiritual practices are very "head-y." This is true sometimes. But it does not have to be. There are many incredibly valuable practices that help practitioners inhabit their bodies. Some of these are quite difficult to share in the context of a book. I hope you will seek some of these activities out, though, and work at reclaiming your body through them.

Yoga is an amazing, embodied practice. There are countless yoga videos available on YouTube. And it seems like every time you look, yoga classes are being offered in new and novel environments like breweries, Nature reserves, and farms.

Drum circles are also incredibly powerful. These are gatherings of people who are coming together to create rhythms. There is nothing quite like the experience of being in a group of a dozen or more human beings, all working together to create a single rhythm. The whole group can feel like one organism. And at the same time, each person might bring in their own unique contribution. The stinging feeling on the hands, the intense volume, and even the feel of the sound-waves as they bounce off the skin are a fascinating medley. Drum circles are often inviting to new and untrained participants. Sometimes owning the instrument isn't even required, as the host will bring extras. Drum circles in your area can probably be located with a web search.

Old standbys like dancing, gardening, hiking, climbing, running, swimming, and other sports have a highly spiritual side. If this aspect of your favorite activity is not instantly apparent, approaching these with a spiritual intent can change your experience. Each of these can also be practiced with an intentional awareness that helps to highlight the spiritual aspects of these activities. If I enter into my gardening with a heart that is open to the fact that I am engaged in a partnership with God and an act of creation, for example, I am much more likely to notice this reality.

Some activities that "look" more like traditional practice help in this area, too. Mindfulness is a discipline primarily composed of practices that are focused on helping people more fully inhabit their bodies. The foundation of mindfulness is that our senses of touch, taste, sight, and smell do not possess fears for the future or worries from the past. When we bring our attention to the world we live in right now, to the data our senses are reporting, we find ourselves in a state that is beyond anxiety and sadness.

Therefore, nearly everything can be approached in a mindful manner. In a sense, being mindful simply means becoming aware of the sensations we receive as we engage in the sorts of activities we do all the time anyway. But of course, if this is all there was to mindfulness, it would not be at the center of a tremendous and growing industry.

## Practice 18
## A Mindfulness Body Scan

- *Take three deep breaths. Sit in an upright but not uncomfortable posture.*

- *For most of this exercise, we will turn our attention to various parts of the body. The idea is to notice how that part feels. Become aware of things like soreness and tension. It is not necessary to try to change this. If you wish, though,*

*when you note something different,*
*you can "breathe" into this space; with*
*the inhale, imagine the breath coming*
*through the nose to directly inhabit the*
*space that feels tense or sore.*

- *Turn your attention to the soles of*
  *your feet and toes. Become aware of*
  *how they are feeling right now. Con-*
  *tinue to breathe deeply, and just make*
  *yourself aware.*

- *Now, become aware of the top of your*
  *feet and the ankles.*

- *Bring your attention up to both*
  *calves. Remember to continue to*
  *breathe deeply: in through the nose,*
  *out through the mouth if possible.*

- *With the next breath, draw your*
  *awareness up to the knees.*

- *Become aware of the top of the*
  *leg. Breathe into any tension or*
  *discomfort.*

- *Notice your lap, pelvis, and buttocks.*
  *Become aware of where you are making*

*contact with your seat. Notice the feel and alignment of muscles, bones, and joints.*

- *Note your stomach and lower back. Continue to be open to breathing into tension here.*

- *Remembering to continue to breathe deeply, draw your awareness up.*

- *Now, consider your fingers and thumbs. Note the joints and the places where they connect with your hands.*

- *Draw your attention to the palms, and up to the wrists.*

- *Notice your forearms, breathing into tenseness here.*

- *Become aware of your upper arms, triceps, and biceps, and where they meet the rest of the body.*

- *Become aware of your shoulders, shoulder blades, and neck. Continue to breathe deeply.*

- *Draw the attention up, to the jaw, face, eye sockets, and scalp.*

- *Now, take three deep breaths. Feel the interconnections in all the parts of your body.*

- *When you are ready, return to your daily activities.*

Mindfulness also offers countless brief activities to bring the practitioner into the moment. One is the countdown: notice five things you see, four things that you hear, three things that you can feel, two things that you can smell, and one thing that you can taste.

Another is to find cues throughout the day that might serve as the ringing of a gong, as a reminder to return to right here and now. For example, on a walk you might cycle through all the colors of the rainbow, looking first for something red, then something orange, then something yellow, green, blue, indigo, and violet. This helps resist the tendency to wander through a walk on autopilot. Typically our default is to attend to the worries of the past or the fears of the future. Looking around for the next color on the rainbow is a constant invitation to be present to this particular moment.

Many forms of contemplation help to turn us off autopilot. Mindfulness is particularly good at this. Mindfulness practices are often more portable than other spiritual practices. While an abbreviated form or an important principle might be lived out in the moment from another spiritual exercise, a mindfulness practice might be done from beginning to end right in the middle of everyday life. Some of them are designed simply just to be a reminder to be present. For example, a practitioner might make the decision that each time they pass through a doorway they are going to use that as a reminder to be aware of where they are, to be present to the moment.

Hopefully, it is becoming clear that the question of "What do I do with this body?" is a deeply spiritual question. There are people who might try to diminish and downplay our physicality. They might even do it with a veneer of religiosity. As we seek the essence of spirituality, we find something rather surprising.

We find that the body is the doorway to embracing the world that we are already occupying. The body is the doorway because the body's physical senses are the ways we find out some important things about how to be in the world.

How to feel content. How to occupy the present moment. How to appreciate so much beauty that would have gone unnoticed.

There is a desire to transcend the world. It is easy and commonplace. And it is not wrong. There is pain and suffering and many things wrong with our existence. I have a hope and belief in a total transformation.

But this desire for transcendence, for leaving physicality behind is not complete, either. This is a good example of a tension worth holding nondualistically. I don't have to choose between embracing my physical presence and longing for spiritual fullness. There is value in me sitting with a tension rather than trying to resolve it. It might even be that I will most fully experience one by embracing the other. If I enter into the particularities of my life this very moment on planet Earth, lived, as it is in my forty-nine-year-old, asthmatic, somewhat out-of-shape body, if I accept and celebrate this here and now, I find out something new about my hopes that live beyond this flesh.

# (Not So) Amazing Grace

I always thought that living for eternity meant living forever, for an infinite number of minutes.

Or hours. Or days. I used to smile and say that this sounded great. Then I heard the less common verses of "Amazing Grace." Have you ever gotten past the first verse? Let me share verse four with you:

*When we've been there ten thousand years,*
*Bright shining as the sun,*
*We've no less days to sing God's praise*
*Than when we first begun.*

Sometimes, when I am singing songs in a church where I feel comfortable, I have magnificent experiences. The music lifts me up and out of where I am. I have this thorough experience of the meaning of all the words. I feel joy-filled. I feel free.

There's only one time I can think of that I experienced the opposite of that. It was when we were working our way through all four verses of that song. In the first three verses, I was into it. I was living those words so fully, and I loved each and every one of them. I was in that altered state, and so the full meaning of each of them was hitting me with a strange forcefulness. When we got to that last verse, I think I was able to experience those words with such a profound intensity that I was . . . horrified.

For some strange reason, it seemed like everybody else should be feeling what I was. It was if someone had put a secret code near the end of one of the world's most well-loved hymns, and the message that code promised was not good. In the middle of that existential vertigo, I looked around. Everybody else seemed like they were still into it. Singing away, raising up their hands. Looking back, I imagine most of them already knew that those were the words. They had perhaps worked their way past the shock of it all. But for me, it added this profound sense of loneliness to the shock and fear of the idea of living ten thousand years and still being at the metaphorical first few minutes.

I like times of worship when it is a community that feels life giving. I enjoy singing to God. There are lots of people in my life who tease me about it. I get it. It's a little bit weird. In that little church the whole worship "experience" would never go on for more than an hour and a half. I could have done it for twice as long though, easy. So three hours sounds great to me to be "singing his praise." But ten thousand years? Actually, no. Not ten thousand years. And then to realize that after ten thousand years, we still have forever left. And it's not just about the fact that we would be spending that end-lessness in what sounds like a church service.

Ten thousand years from now? Let's round my age up to fifty. So a hundred years is twice my current age. One thousand years is twenty times my current life. Ten thousand years is two hundred times the amount of time I have already lived. When I live a span that is two hundred times the current amount of my current lifespan, endlessness will still be dragging endlessly in front of me.

That sounds like hell.

I tried to share this with my friends at the time. They nodded. They told me they got it. But my stomach was clenched in knots. I felt it in my body. It was horrifying. Imagining a timeline. A line that started with my birth in 1971. And it just . . . keeps on going. Forever.

There is another way to understand the nature of eternity. The nature of heaven. It's important to return to the idea that I hold this understanding of forever in a tension with the more traditional view. I don't think one is right and one is wrong. But I can experience eternity right here in this very moment. We have these wonderful experiences where we get a little taste, a little tease, a little prologue of what this might be like. And it comes through our senses. It is the moment when our lips touch the lips of someone we love more deeply than we ever thought possible. It is a timeless time that we lie on the soft sand on the edge of sleep while the ocean spray cools our skin to just the right temperature. It is while we are one organism with the rest of the basketball team, flowing together as if linked by telepathy: there is the squeak of shoes on the floor, the applause, perhaps the smell of sweat, the pounding of the heart. It is the sound of the musical instruments coming together just perfectly, just how it sounded in your imagination but now it is before you, and the song you wrote—it just works!

Remember that timeline? The arrow on the end could be imagined to travel forever horizontally. It would represent a certain understanding of time. Pick any point on that line, and it represents one moment. And our experience could travel forever upward. Imagine a line going up and up and forever up.

But the eternal can be found in this very moment. Forever is right here. It is right now. It is in our body. It comes from a desire not to escape this world and go to heaven. It is a bringing of heaven to Earth.

The theory of the body is important. If the body is just a meat suit, if it is the home to all of our sins and our problems, then the best way of being would be to leave it behind. The goal would be to be a disembodied spirit on a cloud, playing a harp or whatever paradoxical cartoon image you would like to borrow. (Paradoxical for lots of reasons: consider the cartoon angel harp for one. How do those insubstantial strings vibrate and create sounds?)

But if the body is a gateway not a barrier, if the body's senses are the ways we experience the best that there is, then so many things begin to look so different. One of the repercussions of this idea is that of course my body alone is not the only gateway to God. Other bodies are as well.

And the whole of creation is. Every single physical thing is not something that ought to be worshipped just for its own sake—none of it is God—but all of it is God's artwork. All of it bears the Divine signature. All of it is an entryway into the transcendent. If we can see God in anything, we can begin to see God in everything.

The practice on the next page is one that invites you to mindfully take a walk. There, you can witness these doorways to the transcendent.

## Practice 19
## A Mindful Walk

- *Before you begin, have your shoes on.*

- *Sit and center yourself. Release yourself from other responsibilities. Take three deep breaths, in through the nose and out through the mouth.*

- *Stretch, hydrate yourself, and consider your route as needed.*

- *Begin your walk. Focus on a single sensation throughout. You might choose any one of these:*

    *The feeling of the air as it enters through your nose on the inhale.*

    *The feeling of your diaphragm expanding with each breath.*

    *The feeling on the sole of your foot as it makes contact with the ground each time.*

    *The feeling of any soreness or tightness. (It's a strange thing, drawing our awareness to physical hurts. In my experience, doing it casually makes it feel worse. But committing to mindfully inhabiting an ache or a pain is a way to befriend the pain, and realize that pain is only pain.)*

*Looking for a particular shape or color everywhere it appears.*

*Being on the lookout for all the different smells you can notice.*

*Being on the lookout for all the different temperature changes or air movements that come to your cheeks.*

- *To whatever extent it is safe to do so, do not consciously consider the route you are going to take. Dwell inside the perception you chose and let your body decide where you are going to go.*

- *Whenever your brain begins to do its job of thinking, return to your breath or your chosen sensation.*

- *When your walk is completed, spend a few minutes sitting with your chosen sensation and breathing.*

- *Throughout your day today, return to your sensation.*

The body ought to be loved well; it ought to be loved well for its own sake, and it ought to be loved well for what this implies about so many other things. We can tell quite a bit about several other things based on how a person loves their body. One thing we can start to get a picture of is how much they love other bodies. Because we so often equate the body itself with sexuality, it is natural to interpret that last sentence in a certain manner. But once we separate that instant association, we can see that loving our body well might mean we love others well. It is hard to imagine such a person not loving whatever else we are in addition to a body—call it a spirit, personality, mind, soul. If the love goes deeper than lust—if the love of the body is not merely a sexual preoccupation—it will become a love of the whole person.

Further, the love of the body is the beginning of the love of the Earth. Kind and loving treatment of the body is an echo of the treatment of the Earth herself. A person who does their best to be healthy is likely also to be a good environmental steward. It is hard to imagine a person living on junk food and abusing their body would be a good caretaker of the world. This is not just because a healthy person is likely to have more reserves and ability to take care of the Earth. And it is not only because the manufacture of many unhealthy goods is not good for the Earth. Conversely, someone eating and living in a healthy manner is likely someone who is caring for the Earth well. The connections between the body and our planet-home run deep.

# CHAPTER TEN

·❧·❧·❧·❧·❧·❧·❧·❧·❧·❧·❧·❧·❧·❧·❧·❧

# What Does My Day-to-Day Life Look Like Now?

These deep thoughts are all well and good. Ideas are important. But ideas have their limits.

The idea of orthodoxy, that a person must have correct ideas, is a staple of fundamentalist religion. But orthodoxy is about abstraction. It is related to ideas that are not here and now. It is related to theoretics. It is not embodied.

Orthopraxy, which is about right practice, gets a lot less press than orthodoxy. This word—practice—has a wide scope. It runs deeper than the sorts of spiritual practice that are being advocated so far in these pages. Orthopraxy is highly contextual and embodied. It is about the nuts and bolts of everyday life. This is the question of what we do in the totality of life, not only for the relatively small time we might be meditating, but throughout the whole of the day.

This chapter will have two main focuses. The first is on a blossoming spiritual practice. We now have nineteen spiritual practices that have been introduced in these pages. It is worth considering what to do with them here. The second focus will be on that broader use of the term practice: what actions are wise to take during a time of spiritual transition? What sorts of things should a person do?

To varying degrees, the last several chapters were rather abstract. There was a lot to think about. Considerations to weigh, tensions to hold. Now, we can begin to explore some more concrete steps.

I have suggestions to make, based on my experience, but there is power in charting your own course. So l hope that you can carry these suggestions about building your spiritual practice as recommendations about one way to do these things well. It is quite likely you will have a sense about whether these recommendations apply to you. I hope you will listen to the voice within. That voice knows better than I do what is good for you.

My recommendation is that you sit at least once a day six days a week. If you have been doing these practices throughout this book, you might be ready for thirty-minute sessions. Committing to a length of time is more important than the actual length. Using a timer or meditation app is a wise way to go. You might be in the middle of a good session and wish to extend it. That's a healthy and wise thing to do if it is feeling good. However, if you can, avoid cutting your time short; try to at least get to the end of the time to which you committed. Sticking it out is good because some measure of spiritual growth occurs when we make our way through the times that we are tempted to quit. Most of the time, I am thankful that I made it through. If I am feeling antsy or anxious fifteen minutes through, I am likely to be calm and settled when I am done. If I had let myself quit, I never would have made it through.

Many of us find a routine helpful. Using the same space, engaging the practices at the same time, going through the same procedures to get ready . . . These are all powerful things to do. It is fascinating how quickly routine becomes ritual. And ritual can be a very powerful force.

I have taken to meditating in the mornings not long after the dawn. There is a period of time when the sun's strong horizontal rays come shining triumphantly through my window. Each day I continue to do my practice at this time, I feel a stronger connection. Ritual, when it is believed in and endorsed, has this cumulative, slowly growing effect. Sometimes, even if I am not at my practice, when I see those horizontal sun rays I am transported back to it; it is like a sort of short hand that transports me part way into the headspace I was in, just by association. I guess I am willing to be one of Pavlov's dogs if the programmed behavior is good for me!

On the one hand, there are certain steps it is good to take to ensure that the environment is as good as it can be. On the other hand, there are lots of reasons to accept that the environment will never be perfect.

Let's begin with what we can do. Creating a peaceful and inviting environment is a great way to turn this from a chore into a luxurious act of self-care. Light a candle. Get yourself a tall glass of ice water. Make the temperature comfortable. And think about whether you would like to use music. I am learning that notifying the people who live with me is an important thing to do. This is not only because it means that they will be less likely to disturb me, but more than that, setting aside the time and announcing my attention is an act of self-care, an act of declaring my time worthy and this act as important.

Music to accompany a spiritual practice is a mixed bag that of course depends on the disposition of the practitioner. It also depends on the practice, the music, and on how familiar the practitioner is with contemplative practice. Sometimes music can be a distraction. We come back here to the idea that part of the benefit of a spiritual practice is in the ways it forces us to face our fears. Music can provide a place where we can retreat. When facing my truths is nearly unbearable, this relief can be much needed. However, sometimes this option to retreat stands in the way of facing these realities down and growing from them. Sometimes, music can be an invitation into the practice, though. It can be a powerful aid to focusing. If music is to be used, I recommend that it be without lyrics, that it is carefully chosen, and is delivered without commercials to disrupt the flow.

And yet the environment can never be perfect. This is ultimately, paradoxically, a good thing. If we could create a sanctuary that was perfect and impenetrable we might never want to leave. If we could make for ourselves a fortress of solitude that could never be interrupted, we'd get precious little experience with how to deploy these learned skills in the real world.

On a hot summer's day, I had thrown my windows open to get a bit of relief from the oppressive heat. I was pleased to be greeted by bird song. I liked the sound of the wind moving the leaves on the branches. I found these helpful to my practice insofar as I wanted to feel relaxed and at peace. Then, when the inevitable car came by, the driver seemed to have a pressing need to shake up the world with the bass line of the song he was listening to. As I registered these new noises, I noticed a different feeling rising up in me. I was not impressed by the sounds that now entered into my perceptions. In fairness, they were a bit louder than the bird and the breeze. But that fact ought to be balanced by the fact it wasn't around for long. Quickly enough, the car drove out of earshot. Presumably, he was heading off to serenade those further down the street.

When I look at this situation logically, I realize that the bird song and the car radio were doing exactly the same thing from an objective standpoint. Sounds are just vibrating air molecules interacting with certain delicate organs inside the ear. There is nothing inherently different about the sound that annoyed me and the sound that I enjoyed hearing. Whatever differences I was seeing, whatever differences I was feeling, these differences were entirely on the level of interpretation. They rested on me and how I received them. They were rooted in my decisions about what sounds I am open to.

The irritation at the car is rooted in my rather foolish choice to mentally declare bird song natural and car radios unnatural. What sound is more natural to an inner city than a thumping bass? It's practically the sound of the city.

After we have done everything we can to control the aspects of our space that we can control, the next step is to recognize that everything belongs. The next step after that is to accept whatever happens. This turns the car radio from an interruption into something that is not different from the bird song: an expected part of the environment.

This is a process. Denying our frustrations won't help any, so we ought to walk the line between being open to the unexpected without pretending our feelings aren't what we are experiencing. We accept whatever *is*, and that includes our own emotional reactions. When we can reach a place of true acceptance, though, our time of engaging in spiritual practice will be much more fruitful.

We can easily see the world as being hostile to our spiritual practice. I was tempted to see the car with its loud music as something that was diametrically opposed to what I was trying to do as I sat in contemplative practice. This was just another duality to get past. In many ways, this is the descendant of the duality between Sunday and the rest of the week; between the sacred and the profane; between deciding that these people, ideas, and situations are holy and those people, situations, or ideas are secular.

One of the ways it helps to heal this split within myself is to focus on practices that borrow their inspiration from naturally occurring objects. There is something powerful about beholding a slowly changing scene. Perhaps it occupies just enough of our awareness to let us fully engage in the present moment. The practice that follows can be engaged with a candle in your living room. The same mentality, though, can also be used with clouds being blown across the sky, waves crashing into a shore, leaves blowing in the breeze, or even the hypnotic coming and going of regularly placed streetlights as you sit in the passenger seat of a car on a long drive.

## Practice 20
## Candles, Clouds, or Waves

- *Locate the visual stimulation by lighting a candle or other fire, laying down in the grass, or locating yourself at the ocean or beach where you can watch and listen to the waves lapping the shore.*

- *Inhale. Exhale.*

- *Behold the sights before you.*

- *As intrusions enter, return yourself to the thing you are watching.*

Everything belongs. This is a truth that has relevance outside of the time we are doing our spiritual practices. These two perplexing and illuminating words can guide the wider focus of this chapter, as we explore what our day-to-day life looks like during a time of spiritual transition. The activities described in the practices ought to be seen as launching pad, not a destination, to guide us how to enact that simple (and not simple) idea: everything belongs.

Let's return to the pragmatic, rubber-hits-the-road question of what specific things we ought to do. In addition to creating space in our lives to practice these exercises on our own, there are so many opportunities to do them with others. There are many groups that meet regularly and "do" these practices. When you can, getting first-hand instruction from someone experienced in a contemplative practice is powerful. It is likely that you will get better instruction from someone working with you than you can in this book, in fact. (Though many teachers might be a bit more focused on a narrower number of practices.) These might be classes or groups; they could be contemplative worship services. There are two specific groups that could start this journey for you. Many groups of Buddhists and "Quakers" (Friends) engage in a weekly ritual that is quite meditative. These groups might take place online or meet face to face.

As an introvert, I find meeting with contemplative groups to be a particularly comfortable thing to do. I can fulfill my desire to be with people without having the constant pressure to interact in a way that might be out of my comfort zone. It is strangely and powerfully intimate to meditate with people whom I do not know very well, but not uncomfortably so.

There are many things that once seemed quite "secular" or "profane" or "nonspiritual" that a healthy sense of embodiment and mindfulness can make feel magical. We can approach difficult conversations, washing the dishes, mowing the lawn, making love, even paying the bills, as spiritual practices. We could also search for some of the activities mentioned in prior chapters like yoga, drumming, and dancing as sacred practices.

It might be that these sorts of social activities are quite needed. They might be a very important counterbalance to a contemplative practice that is primarily about silence. In fact, a few words about silence are in order here. A few years ago, I would have suggested that silence is the foundation of all spiritual practice. But the more I reflect and study and interact with others, I realize that this is a needed foundation for some of us— and a rather difficult, even toxic, ingredient for others of us.

I am a straight, white, cisgendered male who has identified as Christian for much of the latter half of his life. Many of the aspects of my identity are quite privileged. I have been told that I should speak loudly and often by all sorts of subtle and explicit aspects of the society where I live. It is only more recently I have begun to realize the importance of making space for others.

As someone who was not ever meaningfully silenced before, choosing to sit in quiet is something that was very important to me. It is easy for me to enjoy quiet, and to recognize that left to my own devices, I will tend to be out of balance. My default position is to speak.

One of the reasons that people might transition out of a spiritual community is that they come to recognize that they have been silenced. This was true for me. But the silencing I was experiencing within the community I left was not reopening old wounds. Some of us, however, find ourselves silenced in community and this silencing is reenacting trauma that is older than we are. There is generational silencing going on based on skin color, gender, and sexual identity and preference.

If this is the case for you, I hope that you can find a way to your voice. I hope that you can be loud. These spiritual practices will still have so much to offer you. But while you engage in them, it might be equally important for you to be aware that this chosen time of silence would be best paired with daily activities that help you express your truths. One aspect of the finding of the voice is to dwell in our own lived experiences, to dwell in our bodies, and to pronounce what we know to be no less valid than the dominant narrative.

I am passionate about supporting the institutionally silenced in finding their voices. Whatever I have to offer in this regard, though, is largely theoretical, based as it is on my own guesses about what that experience is like. This particular aspect of day-to-day life, then, I will leave aside for now in favor of some things I am a little more qualified to speak on.

What about the rest of your day-to-day life? What about the twenty-three hours or so that you are not meditating each day?

The bad news is that it will be lonely. The good news is that there are things you can do. The best news is that your blossoming spiritual practice will help you realize that this loneliness is not going to kill you. The pain is tolerable. You will make it through, even while your fears are whispering that this is more than you can take.

As best you can, extending a hand of humility, gentleness, and good humor to everyone, including yourself, at this time will serve you well. Most of us once had the theory that we would know precisely what the next steps are. We had programs, plans, multistep diagrams that laid out exactly what everyone was supposed to do. I figured that I would get increasingly convinced of the rightness of this path as I aged.

This, however, is a time of releasing surety.

I am not here to sell you on anything. I don't want to soft peddle this. There are sometimes I miss how things were before. But there are not very many. And there are joys I experience that the old life couldn't touch. I did not realize how much energy I was spending, convincing myself that I was right. I did not know how many bonds I chose to chain myself with.

# The Temptation of Looking Back

Do you know the story of Orpheus? He was a beautiful and gifted musician. And he was madly in love. On his wedding day, his wife was bit by a snake, died, and went into the underworld. Orpheus wanted her back, and so he followed her. At the end of the story, all he had to do was walk with her out of the underworld without looking back. The dead whispered. The light beckoned. If he turned around, all would be lost. The climax of this story is not a great battle in the conventional sense. There is no swordplay. There are no magical spells. At the end of the day, there is only the question of the will.

It's interesting to me that Orpheus is in a liminal space when this scene occurs. It is not precisely the underworld, nor is it the world above. It is the passage between. This is where Orpheus falls. He can't do it. He looks back. And his wife is forever lost to him.

There's another story I would like to share with you about the temptations of looking back while in a liminal space. Before I do, a few comments on my use of the Bible. My hope is that this book is relevant to people transitioning out of any kind of spiritual tradition. The reality is that many—probably most—people reading this will be transitioning out of Christian communities.

My assumption has been that citing stories out of what Christians generally call the Old and New Testaments would be difficult for many readers to accept. I made a specific decision to downplay specific Bible quotes or stories through the first half of this book. As we enter into the second half of the book, I will use a few. I am not, however, assuming any special relationship or privileged status for the Bible. The stories and quotes I will use are ones intended to be quite relevant to the points being explored here.

The story of Orpheus is similar to a story in the Hebrew scriptures (often called the Old Testament by Christians). As a city is destroyed, a refugee family is told that they must not look back to this place, which is being leveled because of the bad things that went on here. On the road to the town they are headed to, the wife looks back. She is turned into a pillar of salt.

I do not think you are going to be trapped in the underworld forever. Nor is it particularly likely that you will be turned into a pillar of salt. There's wisdom in these old stories, though. They were both told about people in liminal spaces. Orpheus had almost made it, but he was in the transition between two worlds; similarly, Lot's wife had left all the devastation behind her but not yet arrived in her new home.

A pair of almost contradictory statements are at work here. The first is that it is very difficult to not look back. Neither of those mythic figures resists the temptation. The second is that rather destructive things can result when we do. I suspect that these strangely self-contradictory lessons are at work for many of the people who might be reading this book.

It will be best for you not to look back. Continue that movement forward as best you can. Like Lot and his family, the angels will tell you not to. Like Orpheus, there will be spirits that whisper temptingly. Of course, in fact, the consequences will not be so dire as these stories imply. If you are unable to avoid looking back, at least you will know you are in good company. Still, looking back carries with it the danger of being frozen in place, unable to go either forward or backward.

## Perhaps We Still Pray

We have spent some time talking about the ways that we miss our community. This relates to the topic at hand, of course. As we attempt to determine what it is we will do on a day-to-day basis, we must contend with what we will do now during the times we would have been in worship services and other regular time commitments. We have to figure out how we will replace the relationships we once had.

Another aspect of our day-to-day life was alluded to earlier as we explored the loneliness we feel as a result of distance from God. One of the few spiritual practices many of us engaged in, in the old communities where we found ourselves, was conversational prayer with God. There are lots of reasons why this practice might be challenged now. And this challenge leaves us with the question of what it is we will be doing now, on a day-to-day basis, when we once would have prayed.

Perhaps we will still pray.

When I left the church that had been such an integral part of my life for so long, I found a lovely, progressive community. There are two things that I learned at that time that I would like to share with you here. The first thing I learned there was about prayer.

I was struggling so intensely at that time to hold on to prayer. Prayer had once been something I did as naturally as breathing. I never felt alone because I was talking to God all the time back when I first called myself a Christian. When I left that church it was hard to not throw out everything I learned. It was hard to keep up with practices that had served me well. Sometimes, it was because I was learning new ways of looking at things. Other times it was a silly kind of spite. There was a little voice in my head that said, *If I learned it there, it could not possibly be good.*

Like most things, my difficulties with holding on to prayer the way I always had held on before was a mixture of healthy and unhealthy, of good and bad. That new church I found myself a part of had a tradition of finding new and unusual ways to practice prayer during the season of Lent. Prior to that time, I was barely aware that Lent is the forty days leading up to Easter. But I was falling in love with that new place, and trying to work out what I believed about prayer. It seemed like a good opportunity to get connected to that community while I figured things out. I agreed to take part in the Lenten plan before I even knew what the plan was.

As it turned out, it was relatively simple: huge sections of the sanctuary's back wall had butcher paper taped up on it. During the Sunday service, people would be invited to slip back there and write down the things they were praying for. Every morning and every evening the church would be open and those who wanted to pray over that wall would be welcome to do so.

Most of the prayers were anonymous. Some seemed sublime. Others absurd. Some were heart breaking. Others frankly seemed sort of petty to me. Many were mysterious. Each Sunday, more butcher paper went up and more and more things made it onto that wall.

I was there every single weekday morning for the entire season of Lent. Some mornings, I got there before the sun rose. Others, it was just a few minutes before I would have to leave. Most mornings, I was there for at least an hour. Some mornings, there were six or seven of us praying over those words. Other times, it was just a pair of us. But I was there every single morning. And I was praying. Every single morning. Sometimes we prayed together but often we were just in our own little worlds of prayer, each of us doing our own little things.

I was just starting to hear at that time about how important a meditative practice is. I hadn't really figured out how to do any of it. That time in front of those written prayers was my first introduction to actually engaging in prolonged contemplation. I think that's a small part of why that time was so magical for me.

But more than that, that time was magical because of what the praying did for me.

I told you that some of the prayers seemed absurd. I told you that others seemed sublime. I could probably find a different adjective for every single one of those prayers that were up there. I got to know them so well on those cold Lent mornings. Sometimes I would sit in a chair near that wall. Other times I would get up and read them one at a time. I would get so close I could have kissed the words on the wall if I jutted my neck just a little bit.

Early on, there were some prayers that I hovered over. There were some prayers that spoke to me. Some of the prayers spoke to me because I deeply connected with them. Others had such an air of mystery. It was clear there was so much more to the story: hurt and pain and hope all mixed up together. I still wonder about some of those mysteries on our prayer wall. Such strange and cryptic hopes and dreams. I wonder if they were answered in the ways the writers of them had hoped.

In the beginning, I struggled at being respectful toward all the words that were up there. There were some I found silly. Others I found trite. Still others didn't even seem aligned with whom I thought God to be. I didn't spend much time with those prayers that I judged harshly in those earliest days of Lent.

The crisis I was going through at the time was partially about the question, "Does praying actually change anything?" At that point, I would have thought that question was more or less the same as asking, "Does God change the world to grant people's prayers?"

Where I am now, I have to say that I can't say for sure about the second one. I just don't know. I have seen some things that are convincing. And then I realized I was seeing reality as a popularity contest. If I just get enough people, feeling intensely enough about a certain thing, now suddenly it's going to happen? There have been times that it felt like the answer to this question was incredibly important. Now, I am seeing that not having an answer to the question, "Does praying actually change anything?" is quite a different question than, "Does God change the world to grant people's prayers?" That first question, that's the important one.

It turns out those questions aren't the same at all. Because I experienced God changing the world. At the bare minimum, God changed me profoundly in that time. And I am most definitely part of the world. I experienced a transformation! I began to realize how precious little my opinion matters. There were the hopes these people had. There was the desire to bring them to the Creator of the universe.

As I spent hour upon hour with those prayers, I stopped caring about a lot of things. I stopped caring about how it worked. I stopped caring if this was an effective use of my time. I stopped caring about how it could be that way. But more significantly, I stopped caring about my own opinions on the prayers.

Even on day thirty-nine or forty of Lent, I still could have told you what my petty little judgments were on some of those prayers. I could have sorted them into an "in group" and an "out group"—but now I was aware of the utter insignificance of my opinion on the matter. Some of it was related to the vastness of God that I experienced in those praying times. But mostly it was just about having sat with those wishes, hopes, dreams, and thank-you notes to God. I could accept those on their own terms.

At that time, I didn't understand much about nondualism or how important it would become to me. But what I went through was a sort of necessary precursor to nondualism, much in the same way that those long, early mornings were a necessary precursor to formal, official spiritual practice.

We are taking this journey to leave behind what is no longer needed, to recover the essence of things. As we think about what this looks like on a day-to-day basis, we can think about the idea that there might be an essence to prayer and it may just look like this thing I discovered during those forty long days. Prior to that time, I would have seen God as a sort of deeply overpowered superhero. Superman without the kryptonite weakness. God's job was to hang out in some sort of secret base called heaven, and every now and again, when God would hear a cry for help, he would throw on a cape and brightly colored pair of tights and swoop into the world.

That's why it hurt when my life fell apart, and God didn't come in and rescue me in the way I expected. That's why the people who shared my beliefs were able to assume that I was doing something wrong. They (and I) believed that God was the sort of God who did those sorts of things. The fact that God was so good and wonderful and chose not to make a home here spoke volumes about the idea that our bodies and physical location weren't worth much. Believing that God didn't dwell in our everyday life implied something significant.

Part of the answer to the question, "What am I going to do in my everyday life?" is this: "Look for God here." The Divine doesn't sit in a fortress of solitude, watching video screens and waiting for the moment to swoop in. God is already present: within us and in the spaces between.

Two lessons in the new progressive church were relevant to the ways we live in our everyday life. Thus far I have delivered on one. Here is the second thing I learned.

This little church was the first spiritual community I really fell in love with, made up mostly of reconstructing spiritual types. Nearly all of us were transitioning, there. And so we bonded incredibly quickly. We recognized that we were brothers and sisters. Being with those people was like stepping out of a cramped car to indulge in a stunning vista. I made the assumption that this place would be home for a long time. I thought about how I had spent well over a decade at that first church. I was sure I would be with those fellow travelers for at least a decade, too.

But that's not how it was to be.

The group fell apart. There was some drama, but mostly, there was just attrition. And as I look back, I am not surprised. One of the things I realize now is that it is hard to bond a group where there is little in common. And if the things the group members have in common is temporary, for example that they are leaving something behind, if the common denominator is the fact that they are occupying a liminal space, then as soon as that commonality goes away the group might, too.

The point here is that there will be times as we deconstruct where we have nothing with which to fill our day-to-day life. There will be other times that we find a temporary spiritual home we wish would last forever. I hope that it's clear now that building a spiritual practice will help with both. It provides a stability that will carry us through.

One of the characteristics of this process (one that is aided by spiritual practice) is the dividing line between the sacred and the profane. I used to think it was pretty straightforward. The church was sacred. My home was profane. A book about Jesus was sacred. A book about a used-car dealer was profane.

One of the earlier signs of my transition was when I began to find the sacred in some other places: A morning sunrise. A well-written poem.

The perfect balance between bitter and sweet as an iced coffee slaked my thirst on a summer day. It is a powerful act to declare the things that appeal to the senses holy. The things God cares about begins to look like a widening list.

This is why if you find yourself in a group that is not overtly spiritual, that's not a bad thing. If you find the thunderclap of a bowling ball knocking down ten pins holy, then declare the weekly bowling club sacred. If you find the God-like way a deft author's hand can quilt words together to be Divine, then declare the weekly book club sacred. Surely it doesn't take much of a stretch to see defunding the military industrial complex or fighting human trafficking as causes close to God's heart—so you might let the political action group be your church.

One of the ways human beings have tried to leverage spiritual traditions is to isolate their believers from the rest of the world. The world's great spiritual traditions have different ways of reminding us that the here and now is important. This is a golden opportunity. An invitation to enter into the world's worries and concerns. An invitation to assess the things you have been told and to widen your interests.

This chapter will conclude with a breath prayer. It is one that begins with words and gradually builds the silence. Then, once we are in that silence, we explore the holiness of the everyday, quiet moment.

## Practice 21
## Be Still

- *Place your feet flat on the floor.*
- *Breathe.*
- *Think—or say—"Be still, and know that I am God."*
- *Breathe.*
- *Think—or say—"Be still and know that I am."*
- *Breathe.*
- *Think—or say—"Be still and know."*
- *Breathe.*
- *Think—or say—"Be still."*
- *Breathe.*
- *Think—or say—"Be."*
- *Breathe.*

# CHAPTER ELEVEN

# Is This a Process or a Product?

You can learn a lot about a person based on what they believe to be the final goal of spirituality. Some people are very interested in escorting their friends to one specific and final destination. This perspective views religion and spirituality as a sort of product. Others are interested in a process, where the emphasis is not on the end result but rather about how we get there. It might begin to be obvious by this point in this book that I am an advocate of process over product.

Process can be scary. When we don't know precisely where we are going to end up, we have to trust that the world is basically a safe place. There is a reason no one would jump into a hot air balloon over a dangerous jungle. Since we can't control exactly where the balloon goes, we wouldn't want to have it land somewhere we wouldn't want to be.

Believing in process over product is also an act of humility. It embraces our inability to truly and deeply prescribe what is right for other people. For people like me, there is no shortcut to getting to this place of trust and humility. I had to go through a time of experiencing the exact final destination that someone else prescribed. I dwelled there for some time. And I found that it was not everything it was cracked up to be.

Really, how could it have been? What a terrible thing to wish on someone, to tell them that they have arrived. To suggest that the journey is over, that we have got it all figured out, seems unspeakably cruel. What else could there be, for the rest of the life, for somebody who has arrived? I am so glad that it's not an option to be done with the journey.

That said, this wandering spirit can be taken to an extreme. There is something sad about the image of a person who doesn't feel like they are getting anywhere. The lifelong wanderer who never commits to anything misses out.

I think it's instructive to see this whole thing through a metaphor for camping. An individual campsite may not be particularly interesting. Campsites are typically squashed together somewhat. Campgrounds are typically in places that have lots to offer if we venture beyond the confines of our individual site. If a person spent a weekend camping but never left the area of their tent and campfire, they would have quite missed the point of what it is they are doing.

A spirituality that focuses on transplanting its adherents to a final destination, one that is goal-focused, is a lot like somebody who goes camping and then never ventures beyond the area of their single site. In the case of actual camping, the specific site we end up with is arbitrarily assigned by the person who checked us in. In the case of spirituality, we most likely ended up in the "space" arbitrarily assigned to us by circumstances of the time and place of our birth.

A good camping trip and a healthy spirituality begin with a good home base. For camping, it might be site number 27, the one with the nice big tree that provides shade through the afternoon. For spirituality, the home base might be the traditions with which a believer feels comfortable. If the home base is used as a springboard to launch ourselves into the surrounding terrain, we are doing this well.

Whenever I am camping, I have some decisions to make about how I will explore my surroundings. I can study the maps provided by the campsite, much as I might read holy scriptures. I can do an Internet search and explore reviews and postings from people who have been there before, much as I can study the teachings of the adherents of the faith.

There is a part of me that loves the idea of just choosing a direction and walking. There is something mythic in the idea of heading out in the direction of the sunset. I can never know for sure if any human being has ever seen the things I will see when I venture out into the world beyond the paths and roads. On a few occasions, I have discovered some pretty amazing things by doing this.

But I have also gotten lost. A lot. And more frequently, I have been very worried and almost lost. I have ended up with prickers, poison ivy and poison oak, and in scary boxed-in situations from which I have been nearly unable to climb my way out.

But in a strange way, these results are almost preferable to what happens more often. What happens more often is—nothing. I just walk for a while and I begin to get nervous or even bored. I think I have made so much progress, so far away from where I began, but I find out that I have been walking in circles. A series of not-very-interesting views leads me to a terrain that I cannot cross: a wall of vegetation, a sudden cliff, a river infested with mosquitos.

There is a romance to forging our own path. But the thing that nobody often observes about this is that it is hard, unreliable—and often you just don't get very far. At one extreme is the idea that a person might just live totally in their campsite when camping. At the other is the idea that a person might disregard trails, paths, and roads and set out walking with no specific destination in mind. When the first extreme doesn't work out, it's often tempting to jump into the second. Both of these manifest themselves as a form of fundamentalism.

There are the traditional fundamentalists who say that the goal of religion is to end up in a very specific spot. They usually have set up a major-league consequence for stepping outside the lines of this end game. It would be quite strange to go camping and to promise eternal torment to anyone who stepped beyond the markers of this particular site. We might sit at the table, thankful that the scenery we see is so nice. But after a while, we might begin to wonder what would happen if we went out into it.

It is not surprising that a person who thought there were profound consequences for stepping outside of the predetermined boundaries would be the person with the most resentment when they discover the lie. That other fundamentalism often results from the person who feels the most betrayed by the time they wasted being too afraid to venture out into the world. This confirmed and eternal wanderer might understandably end up believing that there is nothing good that comes out of anything that is manmade. A path can start to look like a new form of campsite, just stretched out.

Taking a path laid out by another is an act of trust in the person who laid out that path. And it can be hard to have faith when people have mis-used it in our past. Of course, the more people that take that route, the more wide and flat it becomes. It probably won't take you into that mosquito-infested swamp where there was almost nothing you ever wanted to see. I have been to that swamp plenty of times. Mostly I have returned with noth-ing but pink welts from bug bites.

I do empathize, however, with the person who disdains all roads or paths. Once or twice, when I tried that swamp I thought had nothing for me, I discovered my initial assessment was wrong. I never would have found a particular place of beauty if I had followed the paths. I looked up, and the sunlight came down on the water, or a beam that looked so solid I could build a house around it came in filtered green through the canopy. Perhaps a majestic crane swept by me, or a beaver toddled over by his dam.

I understand the appeal. Just as I understand the appeal of gathering a crowd of good friends within the confines of my assigned campsite. If there are s'mores and beer and laughter and a blazing fire and great stories, if there are hammocks and songs, perhaps even if I don't set a single foot outside my campsite, that's a pretty fine day too.

Over the long term, though, the person who never leaves their site is likely to be as miserable as the person who always disdains roads and paths. Their best compromise is probably somewhere between, most of the time. But please, have your days in the camp site. Have your days of just heading out in a direction, disdaining all the paths. Some days will be good days to walk on the sidewalk next to the roads. Other days it is worth following the trail markers, and even keeping an eye out for that unofficial, almost-path you find yourself. There is a time and a place for all of it.

Just as there is a time and place for following the script that everyone agrees is best. Be the most orthodox of the orthodox. Read your holy scripture, show up to your service. There is a time to venture out onto the road. Follow the path of the person well regarded in your community. Read the right books. Have the right conversations. At some point, a question will present itself. Will you leave the road and venture onto the path? Perhaps you will be prompted by a book written by someone that your community has mixed feelings about, or maybe an activity that not everyone there would sanction. Here, too, there are benefits and drawbacks. Opportunities and dangers. This path you have been walking branches up ahead. One of those options is much more well-traveled than the other. That smaller path that is more difficult to discern, this is the direction of things you might have once told yourself you will never do. It is traversed by the people you once considered "other."

There is plenty of time. There is no perfect route. It will all be fine.

## The Spiritual Journey

A journey is, of course, a process. This is not a metaphor that has been so ruthlessly tortured as the camping one. The journey metaphor is well-known and loved and respected. We hear it used in many settings.

Today's spiritual practice is one that pushes forward the idea of spirituality as a process rather than a product by viewing the experience as a journey. This practice is a visualization: an invitation to use the imagination. Some elements of holy imaging resemble a visualization. Visualizations like this one come across as a bit disjointed when broken down to step-by-step directions. The best way to approach this description is probably to begin by reading the whole thing once through, then return to the first sentence or two. Take a couple deep breaths and bring this image to mind. When it has played itself out, move out into the next few sentences. Be open to departing from the written words or extending the visualizations beyond the end of the words.

Visualizations are made more powerful by tuning into the senses and are made more helpful by overcoming the resistance many of us feel toward them. After leaving childhood, we don't have many opportunities to rely on our imaginations, to give them free rein. Flights of fancy can seem indulgent. Most of us resign ourselves to occasional daydreams sneaking into our everyday life but we may struggle with the concept of intentionally giving ourselves over to "make-believe." Perhaps it is some vestige of the shame we brought on ourselves when we internalized the message that it was time to stop playing "pretend."

I hope that you can give yourself permission to try visualizations like this one and commit fully while you are doing it. If you release yourself of judgement and give visualization a full and fair trial, the worst thing that will happen is that you will discover this is not a good practice for you. (For what it's worth, if you fully commit, I don't think that will be your experience.) The thing is, if you don't give it a try, if you don't allow yourself to go as far off-script as your mind wants, you won't ever truly know.

You don't have to tell anybody. If it ends up being pointless or silly, the rest of the world will never know. What do you have to lose?

## Practice 22
## Beginnings

*Find yourself sitting at a table on the shore of a beautiful lake. It is almost uncomfortably warm. But a gentle breeze comes, carrying dampness and*

*cooling the air to a nearly perfect tem-*
*perature. The sky is so very blue. If*
*you would like, loved ones are nearby.*
*They do not have to be.*

*You get up and look at a stone*
*staircase that leads down and into*
*the lake. Over and around these steps*
*is an elaborate gate, a sort of trellis.*
*Vines and flowers are woven into it.*
*The grass is soft under your bare feet.*
*You walk to the gate and open it.*

*The first several steps are above*
*the water line. The stones are smooth,*
*but much firmer than the grass. At the*
*third step you find yourself ankle deep.*
*The water is only a bit of a surprise.*

*On the fourth step you look up*
*to meet the gaze of a kind teacher.*
*It might be someone you know. (For*
*me, this person is Jesus.) The person*
*might not be alive now—and yet they*
*are here with you. The teacher smiles.*
*You smile. You are knee deep, now, in*
*the refreshing water.*

*When you are chest deep, you are next to the teacher. The teacher reaches out to you with steady arms. You trust them as you lean back and are lowered all the way into the water. There is some fear. It is unnatural to be underwater, trusting in another. The teacher, of course, lifts you back up.*

*"This is my wonderful child with whom I'm well pleased."*

*Where are those words coming from? You cannot be sure.*

*This strange lake does not get deeper than this. You are not meant to go back out the gate you came in, not today. Walk across the lake. The teacher will come with you while you are in the water. He might speak to you. You might hear the words the teacher says.*

*This is the beginning of an adventure. You will return to this shore you set out from. But not today. Eventually you reach that far end of the lake. What waits for you there? Will the teacher come with you? Continue this visualization if you wish.*

The hero's journey was made famous through the work of Joseph Campbell. (Sadly, at this time there is no proven relation between Joseph and your author, but if someone were to suggest such a thing, I would be happy to go along with it.) The hero's journey is said to be lurking beneath all the stories that move us. Many famous stories, including George Lucas' Star Wars and most of the last couple decades of the Disney-Pixar catalog were driven by a conscious understanding of these principles. All of the great stories, myths, and legends can be understood through this lens. Campbell was an expert on world myths and developed this understanding by distilling the elements common to all of them.

The hero's journey is not only an approach to tales that have already been told. It is a way to understand my story. And yours. Like many of the topics we are exploring in these pages, there is not space to do justice to this extraordinary understanding of the world. Entire books and college courses have been developed on this topic. Nonetheless, we can take a quick jog through the hero's journey and find some relevant pieces of wisdom around the topic that a maturely viewed spirituality is one that is focused on a process, not a product. It is, after all called the *hero's journey*, not the *hero's destination*.

It is said that in the beginning of the story our young protagonist plays an ordinary part in his ordinary world. Frodo is just another hobbit. Luke Skywalker is just another moisture farmer. Or you. You were just a Buddhist, a Muslim, a Taoist, an evangelical. Just as Frodo and Luke were pretty ordinary members of their societies, in many ways, so too were you an ordinary member of yours.

And yet, there is something different. The entire village sings of Belle's strangeness. Simba is not just any young lion; he is the prince. Perhaps through his affiliations with his adventuresome uncle, Frodo Baggins is not like the other hobbits. I suspect there is something just a little off with you as well. You're not quite like the other people in your community.

And then there is a call to adventure. An invitation into a magical world. An invitation to be a hero. Young Hamlet is confronted by a ghost who instructs him in why and how he must make things right. Ben Kenobi invites Luke into a world of Jedi knights and rebellions. Hagrid shows up in young Harry Potter's life. A thief runs by Peter Parker. And perhaps there was an opportunity for you to speak your truth to the people in your community. You were sure they were wrong by that time. You open your mouth to say what you have been thinking . . .

If the call is denied, nothing good will result. This is how Peter's Uncle Ben is killed: at the hands of the thief Peter should have stopped. When Luke Skywalker resisted the invitation of Ben Kenobi into a larger world, the only home Luke has ever known is destroyed by storm troopers. And you? If you closed your mouth when you might have opened it, if you did not speak up when you should have, I am sure that ate at you. It was hard, perhaps, not to resent the rest of your community.

Then comes the entry into a new and magical world. Harry Potter arrives at Hogwarts. Orpheus enters into the underworld. Snow White discovers an unlikely group of dwarves with whom she connects. You discover you can leave the community of which you were once a part. The world outside of it is magical, new, strange, and lonely.

Some people seem to be friends and turn out to be enemies. Others seem to be enemies and turn out to be friends. Arthur meets Merlin. The once horrific-seeming Beast comes to appear twice the hero that fearmonger Gaston is. Hamlet's friends Rosencrantz and Guildenstern sell him out to the king and queen. Lucy's first real friend in Narnia sells her out to the White Witch. A tiny and annoying moppet turns out to be the Jedi Master

Yoda. As you wandered your own magical new land, some of the people you once would have vilified turned out to not be so bad. And others whom you try to follow turned out to be scoundrels.

And then there is the conferral of new weapons and powers in addition to the allies. Superman discovers he can fly. Harry Potter gets a broomstick. Frodo discovers that a ring makes him invisible. Jesus is baptized and endorsed by the spirit of God. Siddhartha becomes the Buddha, enlightened as he is at the bodhi tree. And you? There are things that you might have thought you would never do. There are benefits you thought you would never receive.

There will be conflicts and pain. There will be a confrontation, and even a death of sorts. It will seem that all that is lost. But the enemy and the hero are joined in some impossible way. And the death turns out to be something you can come back from. *The Matrix* shows heroic Neo merging with the machines. The last of the Harry Potter movies shows the title character and Voldemort becoming one as they fly about the castle. This will be the climax for you as well: you will die. You will seem to have become the thing you once promised yourself you never would.

But then the hero is reborn. She is triumphant, and she is able to return to the magical world whenever she wishes. She sees that the ordinary world was never that ordinary at all. Belle at the end of her story can travel from castle to town. Peter Parker can go from the streets as a human to the rooftops as a superhero. Harry sadly returns to the Durselys each summer, but he will get back on the train to Hogwarts. And you? You can return, too.

Perhaps you will be able to physically return. Maybe someday you will go back to those services you left behind. Maybe you will rediscover prayer or songs in a way that you can't engage with right now. Maybe you will enter into a new time of hope.

The thing about the fact that the hero now can travel between the mundane world and the magical one is that opens the possibilities of new adventures. It takes us from the realm of completed stories, which end with the words "The End," and into the realm of myth, where the hero rides off into the sunset, giving us reason to believe that these adventures will continue.

You are on a hero's journey. It is a wonderful place to be.

## Cycles and Circles

The cyclical nature implied by the hero's journey is important. We keep coming back to the same things, but we see them in new ways. This is an important aspect of the idea that a true spirituality is a process not a product. The idea that it is a product—the idea that there is a single, final, destination—suggests that this final place is achieved when we arrive at the single true way of understanding things.

There aren't many things in my life that actually work that way. Are there in yours?

I learn something and assume that I am done. I move on, and then, by combining my new understanding with the old one, I find that when I circle back around, I can come at this information in a new way.

For example, I felt uncomfortable when I first read about the genocide, militarism, and violence of the Israelites on their way to the Promised Land. These passages attributed to God some very un-Godlike qualities. On that first reading, I assumed that I had to adjust my idea of God. But I realized that I needed to take seriously the equally biblical claim that God is love. I began to think about the descriptions of Israel wrestling with God, and I wondered if I wasn't wrestling with God, too. In those early days, I was tempted to just throw out my older interpretations and completely replace them with some newer, shinier idea. Eventually, I began to learn that there were good, if limited, things about last year's understandings. They might have been unbalanced, but they weren't completely wrong. I didn't have to start over each time something didn't seem right. I could build on what I had done before. I could elaborate on what had once been too simple.

There is an important principle at work here. It was made famous by Richard Rohr, a Franciscan monk and spiritual hero of millions. The concept is to transcend and include. It is not enough to just grow past a belief, throwing it away forever. There must have been a reason that original belief was so appealing in the first place. There must be something that idea was doing. Hence, an idea must be both transcended and included.

As we circle back to an original idea, we work at including the original understanding. We are not choosing either one thing or another. We are choosing both/and. It's not wrong to say that God is beyond humans so the descriptions of the Divine won't make sense. It isn't wise to merely transcend this idea because we would throw away all of the good and true things happening here. While we transcend, we must, at the same time, include.

A difficult realization is that we must transcend and include even our own spiritual past. Even the places and times that hurt. This is no easy thing. The easy thing would be to only transcend. The easy thing would be to reject and leave it all behind.

But when we get past the projection and baggage and hurt, when we get past our fears and insecurities . . . there was something happening in the place where we were. There was a reason it appealed to us. Transcending and including is not the same as forgetting. It is not even exactly the same thing as forgiving. It is not something you may be ready for now. This is the main job for the remainder of our time together: to resist the urge to only transcend. Let's try to transcend and include where we came from.

Continuing our dedication to our spiritual practice is as critical here and now as it ever was. We can bring the principle of transcend and include even to our search for our spiritual practices that will make up our daily routine. We might find something that works well. But we may also discover something else, and hopefully this something else isn't only different from the first practice. Hopefully, it incorporates all the things we like and adds to them in some important way.

At the same time, it's important to view spiritual practice as a process. It is evolving and changing. There are lots of people, though, who talk about a final destination where meditation might bring us. They might call it something like enlightenment. There are others who find the term *enlightenment* a little misleading; they might prefer to speak about *waking up*. Enlightenment seems to imply that this event happens once and dramatically and is never needed again. Waking up, at least in part, is about being present to this particular moment. Being aware. Every moment brings with it the opportunity to fall asleep to it or to awaken to it.

It is clear that this is not an either/or proposition. Perhaps there is in fact an earth-shattering enlightenment that changes everything. But it's worth remembering the famous Zen saying: "Before enlightenment: chop wood, carry water. After enlightenment: chop wood, carry water." If that saying were formulated today, it might be something like, "Before enlightenment: pass kidney stones and pay taxes. After enlightenment: pass kidney stones and pay taxes."

From the very first words of this saying, we come to expect a distinction. "Before" implies that "after" will be radically different. Before I knew how to cook, I always burned the steak. After I learned how to cook, I knew how to get it just right. Before I stopped drinking, my life was a mess. Ever since I stopped drinking, I have control. Before I met you, I felt so alone. After I met you, I knew I would never be alone again. This is what we expect of a before-and-after: that there is some kind of difference between the two.

We would probably laugh at the dark humor implicit in the situation if someone said before I met you, I felt all alone. After I met you, I still feel alone. If there was a commercial with a photo of a person before and after they started the latest fad diet, we would not be very impressed if the person were the same size in both pictures.

When I take a broad view of most events in life, I realize that I expect them to be sudden and dramatic when in fact they end up being slow and gradual. I expect most things to be a destination when in fact they turn out to be a journey. I expected that graduating from high school (and college, and grad school) would lead to me instantly feeling like an adult. I thought that the day after getting married I would suddenly be a good husband. I thought that the day after my mother died, I would realize that she was gone, but even this realization comes in fits and starts.

It is much more difficult to find a counterexample. It would be difficult to find an example of something that seemed like it was going to be a slow and gradual journey that turned out to be a sudden and dramatic metamorphosis. Sadly, we are not caterpillars about to suddenly become butterflies. Even that transformation comes after weeks spent in a cocoon!

Knowing about deeper things, things of the heart, does not progress in a straight line. Consider gratitude and forgiveness, or hope and love. These four difficult topics cannot simply be taught in some sort of progressive sequence, the way we learned arithmetic, by progressing from adding to subtraction to multiplication to division. With these more abstract concepts, we spiral around in circles, learning first a little about gratitude, then a little more about for-giveness, then perhaps back again to gratitude, then leaping ahead to love, then circling back to forgiveness and gratitude, and so on. If a person viewed the universe in a linear way, this would seem frustrating and counterproductive. If the whole point is to get somewhere new, far away from where we began, this circling can seem like a waste of time.

The next two chapters in this book will explore these four important characteristics—gratitude, forgiveness, hope, and love. Books progress in a linear manner but the process of learning these characteristics is not linear at all. Therefore, as we get better at any one of these, we get better at all four of them.

If I started in my home in the Northeast, and my idea is that I need to get to Florida for a business meeting or a vacation, I would want to move in a more or less straight line to the south. I would want to put miles behind me. I would measure progress by how far away I had gotten from my starting point. If I began seeing the same street signs and other landmarks over and over again, I would feel very frustrated. If instead of taking fast-moving freeways, I took an offramp and began circling through the same neighborhoods over and over again, I would want to quickly get back on course again.

Adopting a cyclical view of things, seeing spirituality as a process rather than a product, as a journey rather than a destination, rejects the idea that the whole point was to go to Florida at all. Often, the essence of what we are seeking was within us all along.

This is the deep wisdom of the hero's journey. We take these great journeys to find out we never needed to take the journey in the first place, because the things we needed were already with us. Dorothy just needed to click her heels together. Luke Skywalker didn't need the targeting device in the X-Wing; he just needed to trust in the force that Ben Kenobi pitched to him in the first ten minutes. Frodo doesn't need sword play and magic to succeed in his mission; he needs the loyalty and trust in Sam that he already knew back in the Shire.

In that spirit, let's close this chapter out with a practice that in many ways resembles the first practice. You might recall that the first practice we did was hardly a practice at all. It was merely the act of sitting with the breath. Now, we return to that simple concept. We have a few more tools in our tool belt, and some different language that will help us to be present in ways we might not have been equipped to be earlier—but it is still the same basic foundational concept.

## Practice 23
## Observing the Breath

- *Create a safe, quiet space.*
- *Sit in a comfortable, upright manner if you are able.*
- *Tune in to your breath. Do your best to accept it without changing it.*

- *Note whether you are using the mouth, nose, or both.*

- *Become aware of specifically where you feel the breath entering the nose or mouth. How does it feel there? What is the temperature?*

- *Extend this awareness of the feeling and temperature as the breath leaves you.*

- *Where does the breath end in your body? Does your abdomen move? Your chest?*

- *When you are ready, increasingly bring yourself into this particular breath. The one you feel right now. This breath, now, is the only breath you can ever change. It is wholly unique among all the breaths you will ever feel. Greet each breath. Find its uniqueness.*

- *Welcome the special breaths that follow in the same way. Sit in this awareness for most of the time you have devoted to your practice today.*

- *When you are ready, return to your everyday life. But know that you can welcome each breath throughout your day.*

# CHAPTER TWELVE

❧❧❧❧❧❧❧❧❧❧❧❧❧❧❧

# Why Do I Need Gratitude and Forgiveness?

Gratitude and forgiveness; hope and love. These four attributes are powerful signposts to cycle past again and again. They epitomize the ways that we keep circling back through themes and concepts into increasing depths. But before we can begin exploring them in a new way, a little bit of excavation is in order. Some reclamation may be necessary. These words are often misused and even weaponized by people who ought to know better.

One part of this excavation can come in the shape of thinking out loud about them, reading these words, wrestling with the concept, and working it out on a conscious level. But this work will be echoed and reflected and enhanced by a blossoming spiritual practice.

It seems to me that this is a bit like cooking. At first, we do the active part: we chop up ingredients and we mix them together, which is comparable to thinking and talking about a certain concept. But eventually, it comes time to shut these ingredients away. We put them in a hot oven and then walk away from them. This mysterious time—this heat, this alchemy—is like the magic of a spiritual practice.

A precise map on the specific course a person charted through these touchstones would be difficult and unnecessary. The path will be different for each of us. What can be provided is some introductory comments and thoughts about each. So, let's take a tour through the countryside. Somewhere in this county is the essence. There are four little villages in that county: gratitude, forgiveness, love, and hope. In this chapter, we'll be spending our time in the first two villages.

## Gratitude

There are many things we accumulate in our spiritual lives that we simply don't need. They are not part of the essence by definition. When we make the decision to take a journey to the essence, we learn that we can discard these things if we wish. They were never important anyway.

Gratitude, however, is not on the list of disposables. It is fundamental and non-negotiable. Gratitude is a simple thing that inevitably gets complicated and weighed down. It can become little more than one more avenue to controlling people. Reclaiming gratitude is an important act. It takes reflection and hard work to do this. If you are ready to begin this good work, I am happy and excited for you. Because this is important work. This is a watershed moment. If it is not time for you to begin here, with the reclaiming of this gratitude, I encourage you to work through this section anyway. You will be back here soon enough of your own accord. Perhaps the next time you swing through this little village, it will be time to begin this work then. After all, sometimes we travel through an area and get out of the car and participate in the community. We let it become a part of us. Other times, it's enough to just drive down the major streets, enjoy the scenery, and carry on to the next destination. If it is time for you to simply drive through gratitude without stopping to visit the many worthy attractions, by simply reading these words you have begun the work.

Let us begin by making sure you have the correct location. Sometimes we are handed poorly drawn, even intentionally misdrawn maps. We are told a place is gratitude when it is clearly not.

Gratitude does not compare the lived experiences of two different people. If someone has decided that someone else's experiences are more difficult than yours and they are holding up that other person as being better at gratitude because they are not bitter, angry, or resentful while you are, they are attempting to distract you and send you somewhere else. It is nearly always destructive to compare the suffering of two people.

If someone tells you, "It could be worse," or, "You should be thankful for X, there are some people who don't even have Y," this is usually true. But it is almost never helpful for someone to observe this.

At the time I am writing this, 7.8 billion people are alive on our planet. Though we may not have the ability to identify specifically who it is, it stands to reason that one of these people is the most miserable human being alive. That person is suffering more than all the other people. She may well have more unfortunate circumstances than any other human being on the planet. If someone said to her, "There's someone out there who has it worse than you" the person could truthfully say (if indeed she knew it to be true), "Nope. I have it worse than everybody else." But what of the rest of us? All 7,799,999,999 of the rest of us could have it worse. Do you feel better now?

Hopefully this tongue-in-cheek counterargument shines the light on something else. Imagine the actual process of determining who the most miserable person in the world actually is. How will we compare physical agony with psychological trauma? More, how will we compare perception with reality?

There are some people who can stoically bear the utter explosion of everything around them. There are others who cannot tolerate even a mild disruption to their schedule. Some people have a high tolerance to pain. Are these people actually experiencing less physical pain? Or are they just better at bearing that pain?

Some of the worst days I have ever had are better than the best days of other people born into different circumstances. My three wonderful children are healthy. I have always had a roof over my head. I have never lived in a war-torn country. But if you pointed out to me any of these things when I was having a tough day, both of our days would be about to get a whole lot worse. Noticing that my suffering is mild and transitory is something I can do for myself. It's not something that is helpful for someone else to observe from the outside.

There's nothing good that comes out of someone else comparing my suffering with another's. Doing this only accomplishes an invalidation of my lived experience. It is a way to suggest that I stop feeling things so much. It seldom increases my feeling of gratitude.

In fairness, gratitude is a tricky thing. During difficult times, it can be hard to find some things to be grateful for. This puts the people who support us in a rather challenging position. If our supporters do not provide any reminders, they don't offer us a form of help that we need in that moment. On the other hand, If they do give us reasons to be thankful, we can hear a note of accusation, a shaming, an implication that we are simply not trying hard enough.

One way to partially get around this dilemma is to create relationships with lots of trust baked into their foundations. People earn the right to speak to our deepest place by investing in us. We learn to trust that people are not judging us by interacting with them for the long term and observing that they are not the judgmental sort.

This is important, because in our most challenging times, if we are not experiencing gratitude, there is something powerful that we are missing out on. One way to get at this gratitude is to disconnect it from the specifics of our life circumstances. What if we did not begin from a place of wanting to be thankful for this specific thing or that specific thing? What if our gratitude was rooted in something more essential? What if we felt gratitude at the most basic level, for the gift of life? What if we were simply grateful for our sense of Something Bigger in the world?

It's easy to see that one person might be more loving than another. Similarly, one person can adopt a stance of being ready to be grateful regardless of their circumstances. There is something critical to emphasize here: a person who does not adopt that stance is not morally deficient. This is not a question of morality. The more grateful person is not the better person in any sense of the word.

Some people appear to have an easier time with this simply based on the way that they are wired. Others, whose lives appear to be easy, may have an easier time with gratitude because they don't need to look very deeply to find things for which to be thankful. But gratitude is not a competition. The challenge is not to be more grateful than our neighbor. Our challenge is to be as grateful as we can be. To the outside world that might appear cantankerous and angry. But if it's less cantankerous and angry than yesterday, if it is the best we have in ourselves in the moment, that is something to hold on to.

One concrete step we can take toward cultivating this overarching sense of gratitude is encapsulated in the practice below.

## Practice 24
## Yes!

- *Place your feet flat on the floor.*
- *Breathe a few breaths. Relax.*
- *With your in-breath, place your hand on your abdomen. Bring your attention to really filling your lungs all the way, starting at the bottom and feeling the movement of your belly.*
- *Exhale. Say to yourself, "Yes. Yes. Yes."*
- *Inhale. Say to yourself "Thank you. Thank you. Thank you."*
- *Continue this pattern for most of your*

*practice today. Try to live the meaning of these words; see if you can gradually enhance the intensity of your "yeses" and "thank you's."*

- *Release these words. Continue your calm and slow breaths. Enjoy a time of union.*

- *When you can, today, return to this breath practice. "Yes. Yes. Yes." "Thank you. Thank you. Thank you."*

---

Ultimately, gratitude is a willingness to look into our lives deeply. It is an openness to the possibility that there might be, in some areas, more than we earned, expected, or deserved. Our lives are so complex with so many components to them. There are likely many parts of our lives that we simply cannot see it, and this may well be because there isn't much there that we didn't earn, expect, and deserve. When we can keep going, keep looking, keep trying to find something, somewhere, we are made better by this act of looking. Like so much of discovering the essence, there is something magnificent about the journey itself.

Balancing, justifying, and reconciling was never what this was about. If you find something, somewhere that is more than you earned, expected, or deserved, please don't let others coerce you into carrying this gratitude into your hurt, pain, and struggles. It probably won't justify them all by itself. It's a bit like a warm hat. When it's wintertime, I will probably wear one. I know it won't keep my whole body warm. I have jackets and gloves and thick socks for the other parts of me. Just because it won't do everything, I'm not going to throw it back in the drawer. This is why a nondualistic stance, built through spiritual practice is so important. Through our daily practice we learn to hold our gratitude in one hand and our hurt in another without the expectation that they are going to negate each other.

## Forgiveness

If gratitude is difficult, then forgiveness can sometimes feel impossible. If it's hard to hear that there are things we can be happy for in our life, even when it's difficult, it may be excruciating to hear that we ought to release our feelings of anger when we have been wronged.

So much real damage has been done by those who would abuse the nature of forgiveness. Many people have been asked to not defend themselves from further abuses. Others have been asked to not pursue some method of compensation for injuries suffered. This is not what forgiveness is about.

Much like gratitude, forgiveness is a thing that can be nearly impossible to navigate on our own. But a background of trust is imperative if someone is to suggest to us that we ought to offer forgiveness to that person who hurt us. Without that trust, the injury is simply compounded. We were hurt by someone once. Then a well-meaning busybody comes in, and in the act of suggesting that it is time for us to forgive, they have hurt us too. They have attempted to bypass the weight and seriousness of the injury that was done to us.

There are a number of cliches about forgiveness, and despite being well-worn, they also speak to the true nature of forgiveness:

- Forgiveness is not for or about the other person.

- Being unwilling to offer up forgiveness is drinking poison and thinking the other person is going to die from it.

- Being unable to offer up forgiveness is giving someone room in your head without charging them rent.

• Offering up forgiveness does not mean what the person did was okay or that you have to put yourself back in the position to allow them to do it again.

In short, forgiveness has to do with the person doing the forgiving, not the person who did wrong.

When someone does us wrong, they have done an act of violence to us. This violence might be physical (perhaps they punched me). It might be financial (perhaps they stole from me). It might be spiritual (perhaps they manipulated me into deeply unhealthy beliefs). The repercussions of these acts of violence usually spreads wide. If I need to see a doctor to heal the place I have been punched, now I might have to pay a financial price to get into see her. If my car being stolen from me prevents me from meeting up with my fiancée, this wound that began as a financial one could now harm my relationships. There are certain aspects of the violence done to us that we cannot undo. A person cannot un-punch me. They can stop spiritually abusing me in the present; they cannot go back in time and take back what they did.

However, we can change something. One of the worst forms of violence is the violence that can be done to our beliefs about ourselves. I want to be the sort of person who sees the best in other people. I want to be the sort of person who helps people heal. I don't want to be the sort of person who inflicts harm on other people. When I am hurt, violence is done to my ideas about how I treat other people. I find myself seeing the worst in others. I want to hurt the perpetrator instead of seeing them healed.

Forgiveness is the choice to limit and contain the violence that has been done to me. It is the hard work of reclaiming my autonomy. It is the process of reclaiming the directions that my thoughts will lead.

## Spiritual Bypassing

Neither forgiveness nor gratitude comes cheap. Some people may ask us to jump straight to them. Spiritual bypassing, however, is like asking someone to teleport around their pain. For better or worse, our pain must be travelled through. This is not a trip for the weak and timid. It is hard to watch someone going through this. It is even more difficult to be the one who is doing it.

Like most processes, we tend to want to rush through it. It doesn't help that others want to rush us, too. They might push us forward because they love us and don't want to watch us suffer.

They also might rush us because they have their own pain and unprocessed baggage that is being stirred up. They probably don't know that a better way is possible. In fact, however, it is all process. It's all the journey.

There is a better way than rushing through our feelings. The better way is not easier. In a sense, though, the better way is quite simple. Feel your feelings. That's all. Just identify and feel your feelings.

When we bottle up feelings, they seem to accumulate a sort of spiritual interest. In ignoring them, we can pretend that they will go away eventually, just like we can hope that a bill collector will stop calling. But the bill just gathers steam. It grows and changes. When it's feelings we're ignoring, not unpaid bills, repression and projection result. They shape the ways we see ourselves and interact with others.

But when we allow ourselves to feel our feelings, we can eventually reach a place of authentic gratitude and forgiveness. We can make our way through and into a new beginning. This is so much better than the fake gratitude and forgiveness that result from trying to short circuit this process, from trying to bypass the suffering.

I would be remiss if I said nothing here about the fact that feeling your feelings is not the same as dwelling on them. We sometimes reach a point, eventually, where we artificially extend the life of our feelings. Wallowing in our emotions is not the same as allowing ourselves to experience them. Navigating this line is tough. It takes discernment and perhaps some feedback from those we trust who know us well.

## Sacred and Secular Feelings

When we operate from the dualistic division of sacred versus secular, we often privilege spiritual matters over so-called earthly ones. So if I am having a conflict or was hurt by someone, these "earthly" feelings are identified as things that are less important than a seemingly spiritual goal like church unity. Thus I am urged to quickly get past whatever has come up between myself and some other person in the community. Similarly, if some sort of positive spiritual outcome or reaction is happening, this is said to be something worthy of my gratitude at the expense of negative feelings about worldly affairs. When we are reeling from the real hurts experienced in the secular world but urged to overlook this experience as intrinsically less valuable than the things that are going on spiritually, this ends up becoming just another form of bypassing our feelings.

Transcending the duality, reemphasizing the "mundane" secular world, is an act that brings new allies, just as the hero's journey promises. This is the strange irony and magic of a journey to the essence. The world we are entering is not one of enchantment and fairies; instead, we discover this "magical world" was there all along, though it was rejected under the label of "secular." Entry into this wider world brings with it access to new experts in the shape of thinkers whose works and talks can be accessed through books, television, and Internet streaming sites like YouTube. You may also find support from psychological therapists. Maybe in your old community you heard that a Christian counselor is the only way to go—but what I found is that these well-intentioned folks were generally quite good on the Christian part, and not quite so skilled on the counselor part.

An even bigger problem arises from the fact that many spiritual communities privilege their own end game and destination over the lived experience of the people who comprise their communities. Forgiveness and gratitude are two of the major casualties here. We are pressured into making a show of forgiving this and expressing gratitude for that, but our individual feelings and experiences are not given the respect that is due to them. Thus a cheap sort of gratitude is all we have to offer; a shallow sort of forgiveness is all that there is within us.

Gratitude and forgiveness are incredibly important, too important to settle for cheap, easy mockeries of what they should be. When the hard, hard work has been done, when we have traveled through the difficult terrain of feeling our feelings, validating our experiences, owning the depth of our loss or anger, our rage or our sadness, our despair or our contempt, we are then, finally, ready to begin the good and important work of forgiveness. It turns out the wider journey we are on, this journey into the essence, is a macrocosm of this particular journey.

The overarching journey toward the essence is a journey of release, letting go, and surrender. We untether ourselves from the ties that no longer need to bind us. We give up this ritual that no longer serves us, or this expectation that is no longer healthy for us, or this community that no longer grows with us. When we have done the work, forgiveness is so much like this wider journey. It is not a new activity on our to-do list. Rather, forgiveness is an act of release. It is an act of letting go. It is an act of submission. But the submission is not submitting ourselves to the person who wronged us; it is not an act of placing ourselves in the same situation again that leads to the hurt.

The words here are much easier than the act. I wish you patience with yourself and the process as you walk down this long road. You are not alone. One of your tools on this journey is your spiritual practice.

We close this chapter with a well-loved spiritual practice called the *examen*. The examen is particularly relevant in matters of black-and-white thinking, which is quite opposed to healthy processing of gratitude and forgiveness. When we generalize into thinking something is all good or all bad, we have trouble naming and working through the specific things for which we ought to be thankful or working on the things requiring our forgiveness.

When we experience deep hurts we can allow this to color our experience of everything. It is nearly impossible to avoid this. When we interpret everything through this lens of hurt, it is profoundly difficult to experience that fundamental gratitude. It is also difficult to assess what actually needs forgiving and where the hurt is located. It is entirely possible that this hurt is just as acute as I initially thought—but if I am not careful and reflective, I have trouble identifying where it started. Left to my own devices, I can let the impact of that anger distort my experiences of so many other things. The feelings diffuse outward, like the smell of bad cologne in a hot room spreading outward from the source, shaping my experience of everything. A few minutes after a smell like that enters a small room, it might be difficult to determine where it even came from.

The examen is a bit like breaking up the day and assessing it point by point. When we look back at each part of the day individually, it can be surprising what we discover about how a few challenging experiences can color our entire experience.

*❧·❧·❧·❧·❧·❧·❧·❧·❧·❧·❧·❧·❧·❧·❧·❧·❧·❧·*

## Practice 25
## The Examen

- *Find your center by placing your feet flat on the floor.*

- *Breathe and relax, as best you can.*

- *When you are ready, bring the last twenty-four hours to your mind. Continue to breathe slowly, in through the nose and out through the mouth. Begin by reliving where you were twenty-four hours ago. Gradually, bring yourself through that last day of your life. Do your best to deeply engage your senses as you relive it; feel the events on your skin, hear them, taste them, even recall the smells.*

- *Consider your desolations:*

  *What are you least thankful for?*

  *Where can't you see God?*

  *What seems to be moving you away from God?*

- *Release your desolations by breathing slowly and calmly.*

- *Consider your consolations.*

  *What are you most thankful for?*

  *Where can you see God?*

  *What seems to be moving you toward God?*

- *Release your consolations by breathing slowly and carefully.*

- *As you consider the last twenty-four hours in their fullness, are there any*

*things you would like to consider:*
*Was God perhaps moving in things*
*you initially labelled "desolations"?*
*Is it possible that God was not as*
*present in things you initially labelled*
*"consolations"?*

- *Release the word-based part of the*
  *practice. Enjoy a moment with God.*

# CHAPTER THIRTEEN

# What Does Love and Hope Look Like Now?

We're still exploring the same countryside, but now we're moving on to the villages of love and hope. First, though, we need to look at some things that may seem to interfere with love and hope (as well as gratitude and forgiveness)— and how self-awareness can make a difference.

## Self-Awareness

Writers, thinkers, and researchers like Brené Brown tell us that we can't pick and choose which feelings we would like to avoid. We can choose to shut down our awareness and connection to all of them, at least for a while, but we can't go about it piecemeal. Therefore, when we try to sidestep our feelings about being wronged so that we can rush straight to forgiveness, this disconnection will not only get us out of touch with our anger, it will also cloud our ability to experience love or gratitude, forgiveness or hope.

These ignored emotions do not go away. Just like an untended physical wound they fester. An infection of these psychic wounds can manifest itself in the form of projection, in which we locate these feelings we do not wish to own in somebody else and make them *other*. We avoid dealing with those feelings for the short term but disowning them doesn't help us get rid of them. Thus it is important to validate the full range of our emotional experiences. We all have feelings that are difficult to admit. This is doubly true if we belonged to a family or community that frequently prescribed our feelings and attitudes rather than letting us formulate our own. It's not only conservative communities that are guilty of this. Progressive communities do it too. (For example, they may be uncomfortable with expressing anger.)

It's hard work overcoming the habits we've established regarding our emotions. I am not sure we ever complete it. But it's good work, honest work, important work. It's the only way to truly become our own person. It is essential for us to know who we are and what we feel. It is the only way to authentically offer love and hope and gratitude and forgiveness.

When we are honest with ourselves, we see that we have a huge range of feelings about even relatively simple things. Sometimes, these feelings contradict. Spiritual practice is critical here. If there is some better way of building a person's tolerance for contradiction, I don't know what it would be.

Psychiatric researchers suggest that there is a distinction between emotions and feelings. An emotion is an instinctive, physiological experience (or state of awareness) that gives you information about the world. A feeling, on the other hand, is your conscious awareness of the emotion. Emotions and feelings can be the same things—but not always. When we don't allow ourselves to feel our emotions, they can remain hidden from us. Hidden, however, does not mean they have gone away.

Buddhists make a similar distinction when they talk about the distinction between pain and suffering. Pain, they say, is mandatory. It's the instinctive response to events that happen in all our lives, things like old age, the death of friends, headaches, and traffic jams. Suffering, according to Buddhist perspective, is optional, however. Suffering is the reaction we have to pain. It's resistance to it. It's the little voice that says, "I can't stand this. This is unbearable. It's not fair. I shouldn't have to go through this."

We might say that pain is an emotion, while suffering is a feeling. And suffering is worse than pain. Suffering leaves little room for gratitude and forgiveness, love and hope. Paradoxically, however, we can choose to respond to pain differently. Even when we are in pain's presence, we can still venture into the four villages of this countryside we've been exploring. We can know gratitude and forgiveness, love and hope at the same time we experience pain.

How we label our emotions matters. As you leave behind the place that was your spiritual home, you may experience fear. But some of that fear is just another word for freedom.

Good people feel all sorts of ways. Feelings don't define us. Even the most heroic people don't lack feelings of cowardice. The most loving people aren't void of feelings of hatred. The most human of all the humans surveyed all their feelings, held the bizarre array in wonder, and chose what to do. My belief is that the people who chose the best— people who made the most change, who did the best for themselves and the world—were people who chose from an honest assessment rooted in self-awareness. They did the hard work of knowing all the emotions they felt.

In the next section, we will explore the very difficult task of loving our enemies. Before we begin, let's get some practice with it. This spiritual practice begins with a petitionary prayer.

## Practice 26
## A Prayer for. . .

- *Find your center. Take a deep breath.*

- *Breathe slowly, in through the nose.*

- *Breathe out through the mouth. If you like, place your hand on your abdomen, and feel the breath coming in and out.*

- *When you are ready, consider the things you are wishing for right now; what are you asking, from God? They might be very specific. They might be very abstract. Whatever they are, bring them to mind.*

- *Consider the people with whom you struggle.*

- *Bring back to mind the things you are wishing for. And pray that the people with whom you struggle will receive these things you are hoping for yourself.*

❦·❦·❦·❦·❦·❦·❦·❦·❦·❦·❦·❦·❦·❦·❦·❦·❦·❦·

## Love

Love enjoys a sort of privileged status. It is the only emotion with an entire genre of stories dedicated to it. It is the only emotion that is said to be identical to God. It is the characteristic that seems to be necessary in order to commit to a partner for life. It is one of the three little words that change everything in a relationship.

Some of us find the "soft" parts of love the easiest. Saying kind things. Recognizing the wonder and beauty of the person before us. Others among us do better with the hard parts of love. Strengthening through confrontation. Saying the hard things. Expecting the best out of the other person. A person who can carry this tension and embody both is well on their way. The religion from which you are transitioning may have privileged one of these aspects over another. This is a vital example of the trouble with dualistic thinking. It is impossible to carry these extremes at the same time if we are operating from a dualistic mindset. If we have to choose between "tough love" and "soft love," we will always lose. We will never love fully.

In the communities that many of us come from, we are told quite specifically about the sorts of things we ought to love. Sometimes it is a little more subtle: the sorts of things we shouldn't love is dictated to us.

Now, in this time of transition, is your opportunity to love the world and all the things in that world. Many of us were not given permission to do so until now. We were told, explicitly or implicitly, that loving the world was inherently sexual, and sexuality is inherently wrong. Perhaps this error arises because the ways we come to know about the world are through our senses. They are therefore, by definition, sensual. There are many things I love through my senses. This needn't be a sexual kind of love.

Loving requires a kind of knowing and seeing. It also grants a kind of knowing and seeing to the other person. If I enter into the particularities of something, if I am fully myself and use all the tools available to truly understand, I often can't help but love. Knowing a thing deeply seems to be a prerequisite to love. I cannot love in the abstract. If the devil is in the details, so too are the angels. To be aware of this particular and precious moment, to note all the ways that right here and now presents itself to me, is to love. Ram Dass, a spiritual teacher adored the world over, has made famous the practice of using the phrase "I am loving awareness."

Love comes crashing into issues of forgiveness and repression with one of Jesus' most excruciating and well-known demands. He said that we ought to love our enemies. If we take seriously the possibility of repression, we start to realize often we do not hate people because there is something hate-able within them. In fact, our hatred of them is truly about the fact that we are relocating—projecting—the worst possible parts of ourselves onto them. If we had truly come to know them as those people are, not as we are convincing ourselves to see them, they would never have been an enemy at all.

Forgive me a nerdy reflection here. Consider, for a moment Harry Potter. (Spoilers follow.) The primary antagonist of this series is well-known: the Dark Lord Voldemort. He murdered Harry's parents, nearly took over the world before the book began, and nearly succeeded a second time through the course of the seven novels. He is genocidal and murderous. There are lots of good reasons to hate him. Slightly less well-known is Dolores Umbridge. She is at first a teacher and eventually headmaster. Near the end, she is part of the overthrow of the magical world and sides with Voldemort. She is not a good person. She is worthy of the name villain. But by any rational standard, her villainy does not measure up to Voldemort's. The depth of my loathing for this Umbridge does not make sense at first glance. It doesn't make sense because she is not real. It also does not make sense because by any logical standard, Voldemort is twice as evil as she is. Certainly, whatever sort of loathing I have for her ought to be at least doubled for the main evil character. Except that I am by profession a teacher. I am a teacher who has in his past sometimes grabbed on a little too tightly to power and control. I am quite capable of demonstrating epic passive aggression. I can hold myself arrogantly. I can be petty. I fear that I can be a sellout. In short, all the things I like least about myself are adequate descriptions of Dolores Umbridge. On the other hand, I have never even thought about committing genocide. I have never killed anyone or led a fascist army to take over a legitimate government. I don't like anything about Voldemort but he is outside of me. I am not threatened by him. Umbridge, meanwhile, has some similarities with me.

If I am to love my enemies, I can begin with fictional characters. But loving Voldemort is easy. Loving Umbridge is hard. She is not real but my fears about myself are. She is not real but the intensity of my negative emotions are. She is not real. Except that she is.

There are some things that we realize are not what we thought they were and we just give up on them. When I determine that children's cartoons are not going to deliver penetrating insight into the human condition, I would not go on a deeper journey to discover the true essence of cartoons. The true essence is fluff and fun. Those cartoons are what they seem to be.

The essence of a true spirituality is not like that. There are so many things that have a certain kind of meaning early in the journey and they come to mean something quite different later in the journey. I used to think loving my enemy meant loving somebody else. The way I see it now? Loving my enemy is about loving me, the parts of me that I would want to project out onto everyone else.

There is a psychological reason to see that we are all one. All the things we notice, think about, and respond to—it is our own self that is doing the responding. We are the common denominator. Reality is not a set of objective things that simply occur. Instead, reality is noticed and reported by people who have limitations, flaws, perspectives, and strengths. I can't meaningfully answer the question, "What happened?" I can only really answer the question "What happened to me?" I don't really have a way of knowing what happened outside of me.

Even if you tell me about something for which I was not present, the only reason I know about it is because you are telling it to me. If that event— the telling to me—had never occurred, then I would never know. Perhaps more important, if I recall your story, if I am able to repeat it back later, it is because things happened in that story that I have decided are worthwhile. If a person we don't care about shares a list of things that strike us as quite ordinary, we would quickly put this out of our mind. On some very important levels, we can never get out of our own way. We are the gatekeeper of our own lived reality. The work we do is fundamentally about us even when it does not appear to be.

This is wrapped up in the importance of love, gratitude, hope, and forgiveness. It's not primarily about unleashing these on the world outside of us. These are characteristics we need for our internal landscape. Have you ever thought it was foggy and discovered it was just condensation on the inside of the windshield? Then you know about this: sometimes we think something is on the outside and really it is within.

But there's more going on than simple projection. I can only experience my own reality—but there is nevertheless a real reality beyond myself. Thinkers such as Ken Wilber have observed that it is somewhat arbitrary, the ways that we put importance on a single individual. We are made of millions of cells. The cells are arranged in tissues, the tissues are arranged in organs. The organs are arranged in organ systems. The organ systems are arranged in organisms. The organisms are arranged in communities. The communities are arranged in ecosystems. All the ecosystems, when taken together, form the biosphere. Everything is interconnected.

We have consciousness of ourselves as individuals, of course. But this seems like a small reason to put so much of our attention on one middle level of this arrangement. There is something to be said for the idea that the consciousness we think is running the show is in fact just giving us a report of the things that are already happening. I grow increasingly convinced that weirdness is baked into reality itself. Love itself might be the force that renders all the boundaries between everything meaningless.

The best way I know to experience this reality, to really live the strange permeability of the boundaries between us, is through spiritual practice. Sometimes this sensation pops up quite surprisingly in the midst of almost any practice. The practice that follows is a good one for specifically targeting these experiences.

## Practice 27
## Connections Between

- *Find a comfortable position. Release your worries and expectations.*

- *Breathe in, through the nose if you can.*

- *Breathe out, through the mouth.*

- *Try to breathe in more deeply. Place your hand on your abdomen and feel it move.*

- *Exhale again.*

- *Take one last inhale, your deepest, before we move on to the next step.*

- *Fully exhale.*

- *Spend a moment considering a plant or tree, in your mind or near you. Behold and love it. Consider the individuality of this one specific plant. See its leaves and branches. Imagine its roots. Allow your thoughts or eyes to linger on this friend.*

- *With your next inhale, recognize that some of the very air you breathed might have been made through that plant.*

- *With your next exhale, breathe the air out knowing this is what the plant will need. It will inhale the carbon dioxide of your breath.*

- *Take two more deep breaths, connecting with the plant in this relationship of oxygen and carbon dioxide.*

- *When you are ready, try to erase the boundaries between yourself and the plant. Can you imagine a level upon which you and the plant are not two separate individuals but one common entity? Experience a sense of oneness with the tree or plant. It is giving you what you need. You are giving it what it needs.*

- *Linger on this experience for as long as you need or want to.*

- *Widen this circle in your mind. See yourself and this tree as a part of all plant-animals within your area. (Perhaps this area is about the size of a city block.) First, sit with the idea that they are in a perfect, reciprocal cycle of oxygen and carbon dioxide.*

- *The gasses, in a way, are just a meta-phor for so much more. Sit in your place in this system. Make it larger, in your mind, if you wish. First, broaden the meaning of relationship, knowing (but don't bother listing) that we get more than just oxygen. Then, broaden the size of the network.*

- *When you have made this network as broad and deep as your mind will*

*allow, sit with it. In some important
sense, all the living creatures in your
mind, all the plants and the animals,
are one.*

- *If you would like, consider whether
  God is present within the animals
  or plants in this relationship. Is God
  above them? Or the movement of the
  matter and energy between them?
  Both? Neither?*

- *Hold this web of connection—you,
  other animals, plants, trees, God—in
  your mind. Take as long as you would
  like to sit as one part of this network
  of relationships.*

- *When you are ready, return in your
  mind to just you and the plant you
  began with. Consider the differences
  between yourself and the plant. Try to
  hold to the idea that you are still one.
  But the plant has specialties. So do
  you. Whatever is formed between the
  two of you is greater than the sum of
  the parts. Think about the ways that
  you and the plant are such a good pair.*

> • *When you are ready to dismiss this practice, thank the plant and move into your day, knowing that you can bring your mind back to your place in this tremendous network of beings.*

Ultimately, love is the recognition that we are in this together. Perhaps it is so small as the realization that I could have been another person if the circumstances were different. Perhaps it is so grand as the conviction that these boundaries that appear to separate us are nothing but illusion. Love is wanting the best for someone else, not as some sort of sacrificial act of selflessness but as a common-sense recognition that we are, in fact, one.

## Hope

One aspect that gratitude, forgiveness, and love have in common is that they are critical to discovering the essence. A growing, mature, and healthy spirituality is one that brings about some evolution to these three characteristics. We no longer see them in quite the same way as we once did.

This is doubly true for hope. Of these four characteristics the thing that I once called hope is the most changed. As we will see shortly, it might be that "hope" is no longer even really the best name for this thing to which we are aspiring.

Once, "faith" would have made the list of the four most important characteristics in my journey. One of the reasons it fell off my list of top four is that some of the things that I would have once meant by "faith" actually come to belong to hope now. Both faith and hope are connected to our beliefs about how the universe works. They are reflections of how the universe will treat people. It would seem that the distinction between the two is just this: Faith is our name for our specific beliefs that the universe is somehow better for us. Hope is our name for the more generalized assumptions that it will all work out for a happy ending.

Because of our faith and our hope, we might have once held to the idea that if a person does this or that, these sorts of results will occur—if we say our prayers correctly, if we believe firmly enough, if we attend the right services with the right people. Whatever it is, if we do this well, then there is a promise for this life, and for the next one. There is the guarantee that even if the world is a battleground we will be protected.

The world is a place of misery, but our actions or beliefs will keep us happy. The world is ruled by randomness, but our actions will keep us in the hands of One who will protect us from these things. Of course, so little of this is verbalized. These transactional assumptions qualify as faith or hope because the believer is expected to count on them, to trust in the future outcome.

I would bet that the single most common crack in a restrictive, immature faith is the disconnect between what we are told is supposed to happen and what we see actually occurring. We know what the arrangements are. We know what we are supposed to believe in. If you are like I was, when you first watch it happen, you assume that somebody must have been doing it wrong. It looked like they were doing it correctly, but they must not be. Otherwise X would not have happened.

If you are anything like me, when this disconnect happens to you, you will begin by doubling down. You will rededicate to the things you were supposed to be doing. You wonder if you need to adjust. So you try again. Only slowly do you begin to suspect that the whole project is just wrong. Everything about it is wrong.

When nobody said these things out loud, it was easy to take them for granted. When somebody formulated it in terms of the group you belong to, it was reassuring in the short term. But when we carry these to their natural conclusions, they begin to seem monstrous.

Consider the idea that *God will protect me if I pray in a Christian kind of way.* It might take a long time to say those words out loud. Probably I believed this for longer than I was able to express this belief in just this way. And if we begin with the premise that some special way of praying—perhaps by invoking Jesus' name—is more powerful than just thinking, meditating, or just sending off good vibes, this is what we believe on some level.

It might be of course, that it is not the way I pray at all. It might be that I place my faith in the idea that God knows if I really am a Christian. I might hope that God pays special attention to me if I am a Christian. This doesn't make things much better, though.

What lurks behind the sentence *God will protect me if I pray in a Christian kind of way* is the horrific statement *God will not protect me if I do not pray in a Christian kind of way.* I don't know about you, but I don't find much solace in beginning with that first sentence once I realize the second phrase is implied by it. This is a pretty dismal reality on which to place our hope.

This is where faith and hope lead us astray. There are versions of hope and faith that are vital. But sometimes figuring out which parts are the bathwater that we ought to throw out, and which parts are the baby that we ought to hold close—sometimes that is very difficult and confusing.

Let's take the example of prayer as a test case. This is instructive not so much on its own terms as it is as a test case, an example of the sorting, explanation, and wrestling that comes up during these times of sorting out helpful hope from unhelpful hope. It is time for me to stop allowing membership in the community to be contingent on how I answer these sorts of questions. I might feel that I haven't progressed very far if I used to adjust my answers in one direction in order to belong, and now I am adjusting in the opposite direction for exactly the same reason. I might think I have worked too hard to be willing to sell out my beliefs now, to subvert the things I believe in order to belong.

I pray often. Sometimes I pray that my life experiences get changed. Sometimes I think they do. There's an interesting body of evidence about the power of prayer: well-done, scientific, double-blind studies. While I hold that evidence in one hand, in the other I hold the truth that there are huge problems with the idea that God only answers certain types of prayer. Or that God would respond based on either the number of people asking for a thing or the emotional intensity with which they were asking.

And this problem of reality-changing-as-a-popularity-contest is not, perhaps the most troublesome aspect of the idea that God waits for our correctly done prayers to change the world. Terrible things happen. They seem to be happening to lots of different kinds of people. In religious communities, hope often takes the form of some variation on the theme of "God will rescue me from this terrible outcome that I am headed toward." There seems to be a blissful cluelessness about how very ghastly this kind of hope is. We know that terrible, undeserved things happen to people. It's not the case that it only seems like the trains were headed to the concentration camps. It's not the case that God made it seem like something terrible was about to happen, but then removed all of the people from their fate. Terrible things really did and do happen.

This means that when we pray to be delivered from suffering, we are begging for special treatment. We are begging to be the one who comes out of the train before it arrives.

Even as I know this, I become aware that I was doing it too.

This book was written during the Covid-19 crisis. When I first heard about the virus, I hoped that it wouldn't kill many people. When it began to kill people, I hoped that it wouldn't kill people near me. When it reached America, I hoped that it wouldn't get my family. When it infected both my brother and father, I hoped it wouldn't get bad for them. When they both ended up in the hospital, I hoped it wouldn't get anybody in my own household . . .

Hope can look like a series of attempts to bargain in a negotiation where we have exactly zero bargaining power. It can be a series of concessions, a series of willing sacrifices. "Okay, virus, fine, You can have foreigners . . . as long as you leave my country alone. Okay, virus, fine, you want Americans too? Just leave my extended family out of it. What's that? You've gone after my brother and father, too?"

When I am at my best, I don't put much stock in national boundaries. I'm embarrassed by how quickly fear reduced me to someone who saw differences between those in America and those living elsewhere.

It's interesting to me how many inward-oriented groups have come up with alternatives to hope. The Buddhists speak of equanimity, a steady consciousness that reality is transient.

The Christian desert fathers spoke of *apatheia*, a state of mind undisturbed by the flow of passions. The Stoics sought after temperance, a balanced and moderate self-control. There are important distinctions among these three ideas, but they share some common ground. And it's no accident that these three groups that found it necessary to find alternatives to hope each possess a proud tradition of contemplative practice.

Going inward—contemplation—is about facing up to your fears. This is in some ways the exact opposite of hope. At first glance, hope is about believing that the worst thing isn't going to happen. Contemplatives learn that maybe the very worst thing will happen, and sometimes the very worst thing does. But usually when it does, we are still here on the other side of it. And if we are not? Well, in that case, the problem has also sorted itself out.

This is not fatalism. In a subtle and profound way it takes defeatism and turns it on its head. This is not a trivial abstraction. There is a life-changing difference in this attitude change. I remember when I first began to grasp it.

There are some ways that I was not very well-suited for my day job when I began. The people who knew me found it quite shocking that I was on my way to try to teach behaviorally challenged, physically aggressive adolescents. I am not a physical or confrontational person. Despite this, over my career, I have been trained in four different methods of physical restraint. I have worked in environments where I have engaged in multiple restraints in a day. Early in my career, I worked in a facility that utilized twelve-point leather restraint straps to essentially tie down students who posed a danger to themselves and others. I have been assaulted countless times. I have broken up fights, been involved in near-riot situations. I spent about a month out of work with a sprained back and have had to go to medical clinics or emergency rooms numerous times. Sometimes the system has worked like it was supposed to. It minimized risk and trauma to all involved. Other times it has not.

When I started in the field, I operated from a space of fearfulness. At that time, every day I would have hopes. I would hope that there wouldn't be some sort of physical altercation. I would hope that I wouldn't be scared. I would hope that I wouldn't get hurt.

The disappointment of having those hopes dashed was so painful that I gave up on them. But I didn't just release them. I grabbed my hopes and beat them to death. (Kind of ironic, I suppose. I was angry and violent with the very contents of my mind because I was distressed by the fact that the world outside of me was angry and violent.)

I remember the upset stomach I would get on the drive up the hill to the school. I would end each day and wonder if I would come back the next day. But I did.

It didn't take that many horrible moments to birth that fear. Each time my hopes were dashed contributed to my state of fear. Like the times when I would radio for support and the support wouldn't come because we were short staffed. Times when the class would go for hours just barely contained, hovering on the edge of going to hell in a handbasket, where I felt like if I breathed wrong, that would be the straw that broke the camel's back and everything would just fall apart.

The end of the day was the worst time. (It pretty much always is in special education.) We would send kids to homerooms based on the spe- cific destination where  they were headed. We would lose the group that we worked with for hours each day and end up with an anxious and tired crew that we only saw for a few minutes every day. The thing about working with troubled kids is that they generally don't care about the rules even when they do understand them. It is all about relationships. And you don't have relationships with kids you only see for fifteen minutes a day.

One day I began to learn about hope and its alternatives. We were in homeroom, and one student I did not know very well was doing something he shouldn't. I told him I would need to report his behavior to the residential staff if he continued. He continued. (I would have done well to remember my own advice and rely on our relationship, not the rules in that situation. I wasn't really a rookie then, but let's call this rookie mistake #1.) Eventually, we got to the end of homeroom. He was about to be taken off my hands. In the short term, it would have been easier to not rock the boat but by that point, I knew enough to know that if I didn't follow through with the commitment I had made to this student and to myself, neither he nor I would respect me later. I reported the negative behavior to the residential staff.

This was a big deal. Staff in the residences did their best to support us and follow through with consequences for behavior during the school day. The staff member came in the door and I turned to face him, putting my profile to this student. (That was rookie mistake #2.) I was so excited the disruptive student was about to be taken off my hands, and so proud of myself for following through with what I said I was going to do, my attention was completely on the other adult. (And let's just call that rookie mistake #3.)

Before I could get a complete sentence out, the student punched me hard in the side of the neck. At least that is what people told me later. They tell me I dropped to the ground and took a good minute or two to open my eyes. All I knew was that suddenly I was on the floor looking up at everyone. That was not a good day.

Except that it was.

There came a point not long after that, in the middle of my work difficulties and challenges, when I felt my fear begin to rise up again. But then a calmness came through me, a deep realization saying, "The worst thing that can realistically happen is you're going to get hurt. And you've already been hurt: knocked out, out of work, sore, bruises. It wasn't fun. But you made it through. You're going to be fine."

I would have saved myself some suffering if I had been able to generalize this lesson to the rest of my life outside my job. A few years later when my life fell apart, I developed an anxiety disorder. I experienced every little whispering of the possibility of things that could go wrong as a wildfire that lit up my inner landscape. In these terrible make-believe scenarios, one little event would trigger a second and a third and a fourth, and the chain reaction would bury me.

On some levels, it was a rational fear. Because that was what had already happened in life. A series of cascading unfortunate events and challenges fed one on another in an unlikely and devastating series of challenges. By going through that, I learned that this was the sort of world where bad things can happen. Hope doesn't save us. Membership in the right group doesn't save us. Saying prayers the right way doesn't save us.

But there were two important things these daymares left. The first was that in roughly forty years, circumstances had conspired to do such devastating damage in my life exactly once. The more important omission from these fears was the epilogue to that huge mess: somehow I had made it through all those terrible things. Many aspects of my life stayed the same through this difficult time. Even some of the things I loved best stayed the same, but I was now too fearful to enjoy the things I had left.

Things began to turn around for me when I was able to face these potential catastrophes and realize that I had made it through events virtually identical to them before. It only stood to reason that I would make it through them again. When I stopped hoping that the world was a kind and easy place, and recognized that the world is the kind of place where incredibly good and bad things happened, sometimes without much rhyme or reason, and when I realized that people made it to the other side of the vast majority of these, I began to heal.

It's tricky to see how this recognition of the fact that things can end up going badly is not akin to despair. It is not desolation. It is not a state of hopelessness. It ends up being a wellspring of living with authentic positivity, despite the appearance. One of the reasons for this is because I am not constantly having to play some form of pretend with myself. I am not having to constantly rationalize how the things I am seeing fit in with my hope that things will be nice. Because I am honest with myself, when things are not nice, it comes as no big shock.

My early experiences in this came from actually living through some difficult events. This seems to be the way of things, at least for me. The first few times I learn the hard way. Slowly, I begin to generalize.

But if I had only these lessons to build on, I would have only gone about halfway. This way of handling life's challenges comes to a sudden stop at a point. There's another truth to hold in the midst of all this.

I am going to die someday.

You are going to die someday.

We are all going to die someday.

Death comes quickly for some of us. It comes slowly for the rest. Slowly means, in a sense, that it comes after a series of worst-case scenarios. My education in knowing what to do with hope would have been incomplete if I had only gone through those two events: first the student knocking me out and then life falling apart. In both those situations, I was still standing after it was all over. I wasn't dead.

Hope begins in the knowledge that if life is constant change, then it must follow that no situation is forever. Tomorrow can be—and often will be—different from today. Hope finds its fulfillment in the reality that there are very few outcomes we cannot come back from. We can almost always try again, try differently, try something new.

For many of us, early on, we identify only one thing that is good and we delude ourselves into thinking we can have only that one thing. We think, for example, we can have hope and faith, and banish the other things that pop up with them. We think we can fully embrace these without having to contend with things like doubt. That which inevitably emerges, those things that almost seem like opposites to the values we are holding, are sometimes called shadows.

It's easy to miss the brilliance of that particular choice of words. Calling it a shadow is perfect. Imagine a person standing outside in the late afternoon. The sun is a good piece of the way toward setting. Could you ever escape your shadow? Only by entering into the darkness.

In discovering the essence, we discover that we can't have hope without doubt. Pushing it away and pretending it is not there will only make it stronger. This is equally true of the other three characteristics we have been exploring in these last couple chapters. The opposites to love, gratitude and forgiveness will inevitably arise.

So, there will be hard—and good—work ahead. Much of this work will be around finding kindness for ourselves and for others. It is at times like this that the Buddhist Tonglen practice can be useful.

# Practice 28
## Tonglen

- *Place your feet flat on the floor. Breathe slowly through your nose and out through your mouth. Fill your diaphragm with your in-breaths. It can be helpful to place the hand on the abdomen as you do this, to feel its movement.*

- *When you are ready to begin this practice in earnest, breathe in feelings of heaviness, claustrophobia, pain, and hurt. Do not assign this to any experience or person yet.*

- *Breathe out positivity, light, and joy.*

- *With your next in-breath, experience the unpleasantness as entering into you through all the pores of your body. Feel it come along with your breath and travel within.*

- *When you exhale positivity, feel this emanating from your pores, as well as your breath. Envision this goodness going out into the world.*

- *Continue this process for a while.*

- *When you are ready, call to mind a particular situation that is difficult and painful. Apply your imagination to the experience you have chosen. Take into yourself the pain and hurt from the person or group involved. Take it through the breath and through the body.*

- *Exhale whatever relief you feel is best: kindness, light, and joy.*

- *Continue to inhale the situation's pain. Exhale relief.*

- *As your practice draws to a close, widen your compassion. If you can, take on the pain in a more intense manner, or feel it coming into you from a wider circle.*

- *Continue to exhale love to this widened, deepened circle.*

- *When you are ready to release your day's practice, spend some time continuing to breathe. Consider what the experience was like of feeling others' pain.*

# CHAPTER FOURTEEN

# What Is the Role of Suffering and Dying?

*THUNK! Thunkthunkthunkthunk.*
My wife and I looked at each other fearfully. "We better check it out." I said. "Why don't you take the next offramp."

I am not an idiot; neither is my wife. We had both had flat tires before. We should have known. This was several years ago, though, when I was still operating from a traditional view of hope. It was a hot summer day, and things in my life were about to get very complicated. We couldn't afford roadside assistance. We couldn't afford a new tire.

We had our three tiny kids crammed in their car seats in the back. So we hoped for the best.

We got off on what is surely Massachusetts' longest offramp. The sound morphed; it took on a grinding note. We knew what it was. There was absolutely no reason to drive that far on a flat. But I grasped on to the possibility that maybe there was something like cardboard stuck in the wheel that I would just be able to pull out. It's not that I had any good reason to suspect that this was the culprit. The sound didn't sound anything like that. I hadn't seen anything before it all started. But hope, stupidly, springs eternal.

At that moment in my life, there were more problems and fears dominating my world than I would have been able to name. Mental health struggles. Parenting insecurities. And of course, money, money, money. The finances were a symptom and a cause of our problems; the lack of money prevented us from solving many of the other ones, and the huge stress levels prevented me from attaining the discipline that would have nudged our finances in a more healthy direction.

By the time we pulled over, there was nothing left of the tire. And my life was about to get much worse. Within a few months of that time, I would begin to struggle with anxiety and depression. Within less than a year, I would be nearly debilitated by these challenges. It was not my finest hour as a father, husband, teacher. Therapy and medication were huge assets in my recovery. They were incredibly necessary first steps. But they weren't enough by themselves.

I don't know if it was God's hand or dumb luck that led me to discover contemplative practice at this time. Contemplative practice was the necessary next step for me. Contemplative practice taught me what to do with my fear. It taught me to face down the highly unlikely negatives so that I could deal realistically with the much more likely challenges I would face. It taught me to use hope in a way that had a positive impact in my life. Using hope in the right way, for example, would have enabled me to identify that *thumpthumpthumpthump* was a flat tire, even as much as I didn't want it to be.

At that time, however, I was not equipped to face reality. I was unable to enter into the fullness of the moment because I had not yet truly experienced the idea that there is more to me than just the moment. If the moment before me was scary, I couldn't see anything beyond that fear. If it was fear-filled, I felt taken over by the fear. If there was loss, I couldn't find myself amidst all that loss.

So when I knew that the tire had gone flat, truly knew it, I didn't have much sense of self left, beyond that big, scared, overwhelmed feeling. There wasn't enough of me left to solve the problem. As I write these words, I am thinking about those animals that change their colors to match their surroundings. I was like one of those. Except that if I had been one of those animals back then, I would have looked down at my perfectly camouflage body and wondered, in fear, "Where am I?" I would have lamented, "I have disappeared!"

# Accepting Suffering

Left to my own devices, when I am not using the things I have learned in meditation, when I am angry, I come to identify myself with my anger. When I am hurt—whether it is a physical or emotional pain—I see little of myself beyond that pain. When I am lonely, I come to think that I am the loneliness itself. When I am suffering I see so little of myself beyond that suffering. When I am afraid, that fear is so omnipresent that I feel swallowed whole by it; I see nothing of myself outside of that fear.

It became natural, then, to wish to disconnect myself from the suffering, in whatever form it arose, by distracting myself. If I am experiencing loneliness, I remind myself that there is more to me than just that.

Contemplation has taught me to dwell in my suffering. Not forever. Not even for an hour. But for a while. A few minutes. Half an hour, maybe. Even something physical, like a headache, can be managed in this way. When I stop running from the hurt and spend a moment occupying that space, I realize that it is not as bad as I thought it was. I suspect the energy I put into trying to shield myself from this makes it worse, not better. I also become aware, once again, that suffering doesn't kill me. It simply is what it is.

So when I explore my loneliness, there are other parts of me. They are directing myself back to this place. I am reminded that I am not my suffering, that this suffering is only an experience I am having, because I have enlisted something that can stand over the loneliness and behold it. I can watch my suffering with interested compassion and in doing that I learn that I am so much more than it.

Anchoring myself to my present, lived reality through tuning into my sensory information changes my perspective. Now I'd like to introduce you to one of the last spiritual practices I will be sharing with you. Like mindfulness itself, this practice is also a gift from Buddhism.

# Practice 29
# The Five Remembrances

- *Place your feet flat on the floor. As best you can, relax.*

- *With your next inhale, think the first remembrance: I am of the nature to grow old. There is no way to escape growing old while I live.*

- *For the exhale, and the whole next breath, embrace this reality.*

- *With your next inhale, think the second remembrance: I am of the nature to have ill health. There is no way to escape ill health sometimes.*

- *For the exhale and the whole next breath, embrace this reality.*

- *With your next inhale, think the third remembrance: I am of the nature to die. There is no way to escape death.*

- *For the exhale and the whole next breath, recognize this truth.*

- *With your next inhale, embrace the*

> *fourth remembrance: All that is dear to me and everyone I love are of the nature to change. There is no way to escape being separated from them.*

- *Exhale and breathe your next breath. And accept this reality.*

- *With your next inhale, acknowledge this, the final Buddhist remembrance: My actions are my only true belongings. I cannot escape the consequences of my actions. My actions are the ground upon which I stand.*

- *Release these words and sit in the truth that you are facing. Hopefully you feel freed by this.*

## Accepting Death

When my mother was dying, I found a wonderful, progressive church composed mostly of deconstructing folks. This is the church where I experienced the prayer wall at Lent. It is the community that would eventually implode, due to the differing directions our spiritual transitions lead us. Before the implosion, though, our wonderful pastor watched me process my mom's death at the same time I was struggling with so many Big Things. He had the wisdom and insight to see that I was ready for something more. The pastor of that church helped me make arrangements to get me away for a week to a male rite of passage.

Rites of passage would have been traditional parts of growing up in many societies. They would have been often experienced by adolescents, on the verge of adulthood. There is a belief (one which I heartily endorse!) that many of our societal problems in general, and toxic masculinity in particular, are a result of this lack. Men don't experience menstruation or childbirth, and as a result, we lack a script for how to handle situations that are out of our own control. Rites of passage provide such a script.

Later, I would tell the pastor, "You know, I thought we were going there to play with sparklers. But you bastards lit me on fire." He was the sort of pastor you could call a bastard. There aren't too many pastors I have known that I would say that about. He knew me pretty well. He saw (I think and I hope) that I didn't really mean this as a criticism. It was a statement about the gulf between what I expected and what had actually happened.

The rite of passage was powerful and intimate, more so than I can describe in words. I went through a ritualistic death, which left me with the realization that the worst thing that can possibly happen is that I will die. In a very real way, I experienced this ritual as an actual experience. I died—and I came back from it.

In reality, this wasn't my first death. In a way a part of me died when my mother did. I also died when my life fell apart. When I left the church. When my first girlfriend ever dumped me. When my parents divorced. When I was an infant and realized I wasn't God. All these deaths were unacknowledged at the time. My ritualistic death at the rite of passage reached across each of these deaths and tied them all together. I experienced death—and then I continued to live.

My survival of each of these deaths is part of why I believe in resurrection. My experience of the ritual of reaching across space-time carried this new understanding of what Jesus' crucifixion means. Watching life emerge in the spring also does that for me. So does understanding the carbon cycle. So does learning about the lives of stars and the evolution of the entire universe. All these lives, deaths, and resurrections together sing the same song. They tell me the same truths. The ritual I experienced allowed me to die so that

I could have that visceral experience of making it to the other side, accompanied by elders who could name it with me. It was an experience that was larger than literal truth.

This in turn, paves the way for who I am, now, and how I feel about religion. Once religion was my literal truth. Then it was a lie. And now? My experience reaches out of ordinary time and brings everything together in a way that I can only describe as larger than literal truth.

I believe in the power of resurrection. I believe the world is good and that our physicality is a prime aspect of who we are. I believe in engagement with politics. I believe in love. I believe in the power of a contemplative stance. I have learned to allow myself rest, relaxation, and pleasure. Some of this is rooted in learning to love the physical world. It is about allowing myself to live fully in this particular moment. It is about loving myself enough to let enjoyment be an experience just for the sake of enjoyment.

I don't have much interest in deciding which box I fit in. Sometimes others find it easier and safer to be able to know how and where to categorize me. If somebody feels that need, I find that the words that describe me best are Christ-centered mystic.

I am more humble and tentative than I once was. Part of the thing about seeing all of this as a process is that the act of learning is much more important than the particular things I might be learning. I believe that gradually we get increasingly honed in on the truth, but that we will never be one hundred percent there.

I find value in looking into scripture to get a sense of the flowing narrative. The scripture that happens to speaks to me most viscerally is contained in the Christian Bible. The act of working out what is true is a holy act. The individual verses are not as interesting to me. I am not interested in arguing, generally speaking, and I reject the idea that an argument might be settled by referring to a single out-of-context verse.

I currently attend and love a weekly dinner church. It is progressive in orientation and Methodist in terms of funding. Each week we come together in a closed café and begin with a quick song or moment of contemplation. We pass a loaf of bread and participate in the first half of the eucharist. We sing songs, pray for each other, and participate in a sermon-discussion hybrid. At the end of the service we pass grape juice, completing the communion ritual. It's weird for Sundays not to be my days to practice organized religion. But good-weird.

My family has put itself back together over these years. That doesn't mean that the mental health challenges have gone away. But we know how to deal with it together now. I meditate for about half an hour a day on weekdays. Over the weekend I aim for an hour.

It's kind of ironic. At one point in my journey, I wanted to find common ground with the other world religions by finding a place where they all pointed at the same thing. I spent a lot of money and time learning from the best and the brightest. All my heavy thinking didn't give me a very satisfactory result. Through my quiet times, however, taking an inner adventure, I have actually found that common ground. I see it in the writing of the mystics of every spiritual tradition. In essential ways, we are all playing the same game. This is one of the many ways I have learned that lived experience and emotional realities are often more helpful than intellectualization and philosophical posturing.

## Ecstatic Experiences

Almost half the time meditation and prayer is something I quite enjoy. Almost half the time it does feel like work. But every now and again? There are these ecstatic experiences.

I have mixed feelings around talking about ecstatic experiences. My hesitation is partially rooted in a bit of selfishness. Putting these transcendent events into words can cheapen them. But part of my hesitation is more than this; I am deeply aware that not everyone will experience these. I would not wish to set them up as the goal of meditation, nor would I imply that those who do not have them are somehow doing it wrong.

These things don't happen very often but when they do, they are delicious. Often, they are almost too much. Like when you are eating from a box of truffles and after the first one or two bites, a part of the brain declares it has had enough of the decadence. When I have these experiences, I get a sensation that feels like all the pleasure centers of my brain are on overdrive, all the neurotransmitters for positive sensations operating at once. I usually have very little sense of my own boundaries. I feel at one with God, at one with humanity, and strangely even reconciled to my own self and all the parts of me. I don't feel like something you could literally or intellectually dissect. I am no longer separate from the whole rest of the cosmos, and all the parts of "me" that someone might want to differentiate between—body and soul, mind and spirit, arms and legs, all of it—feels like one seamlessly integrated unit that could never be disentangled from the rest.

These rather rare experiences have shaped my views in a variety of ways. I feel closer to the people around me after them. I have a lived experience of something to work toward in my own personal development. It has shaped my view of our cosmic destiny and the nature of all things. Partially as a result of these experiences, I believe that I will return to God one day.

There is a substantial negative to all this that is particularly worth mentioning in a book that strongly pitches building a spiritual practice. At the end of the day, despite how wonderful these experiences are, I find myself sometimes wondering if they are worth it. Because the negative temptation they carry with them is substantial.

Hopefully, it is clear by now that an important aspect of spiritual practice is accepting this particular moment, just as it exactly is. Being present to the realities of the things that are right here and right now is crucial. All the ecstatic experiences I have ever had began there, in a radical acceptance of the circumstances that were in my life right in that moment. My ability to be fully in the moment in a manner that is almost timeless helped these experiences along. They enhanced my enjoyment of them. In a subtle way, I think they helped create a sort of chain reaction.

To varying degrees, however, I often lost this ability to embrace the full newness of each moment in the aftermath of ecstatic experiences. Despite the fact that some part of me knows that living in the past is the opposite of engaging in contemplation, I cannot help but try to recreate the experiences that lead to that particular place of wonder. My wisest self knows that the most important part of the original experience was precisely that I wasn't living in the past when I had the initial experience; much of the wonder lies in the fact that it is new, fresh, and right there.

When I began to have ecstatic experiences, I loved them—but I found myself surprised and frustrated with the anticlimax that came later. I would go from an amazing session to a dry, stale, and difficult one. But once I started to grasp this phenomenon, it changed. I went through a period of not experiencing them much at all. When they began to come on I would feel quite conflicted. I saw what was coming. My trepidation cut short some of these times. I am sure I completely cut off other events before they even began at all.

These days I am doing better. I am not perfect at it. But I am practicing at disinvesting myself from the outcome. This is a good thing to practice. It began when I was willing to see ecstatic experiences nondualistically: I recognized the good sides and the bad sides without a desire to resolve them. On the one hand, I can enjoy an ecstatic experience. On the other, I recognize that emotional perceptions were never the point at all. In so many ways, contemplative practice becomes more than a metaphor for the way we live the rest of our lives. It becomes an object lesson and an icon. This is a deepening of my learning about hope.

At this point I'd like to offer up a practice that looks directly at the possibility of union with God. St. John of the Cross said, "The soul that is united and transformed in God breathes God in God with the same Divine breathing, with which God, while in her, breathes her in."

## Practice 30
## A Soul United

- *Take three deep and cleansing breaths.*

- *Begin with the knowledge that your soul is breathing the very substance of God.*

- *Inhale the very material that forms God.*

- *Exhale the very stuff that forms God.*
- *Repeat these breaths two more times.*
- *As you hold this knowledge that the soul is breathing God into you, know that you are surrounded by God.*
- *Inhale, knowing that you are in God just as a fish is in the sea.*
- *Exhale, knowing that you are in God just as a fish is in the sea.*
- *Repeat these last two steps two more times.*
- *For three breaths, hold both sides of that equation: You are in God. God is in you.*
- *Now, know that God breathes. The God outside of you breathes.*
- *Inhale, knowing that God breathes just like that.*
- *Exhale, knowing that God breathes just like that.*
- *Repeat these last two steps two more times.*
- *With your next inhalation, visualize, again, how you breathe in God.*

- *With your next exhalation, visualize, again, how you breathe out the very stuff of God.*

- *Now, know that just as you breathe in God, God-outside-of-you is breathing in the very stuff of you.*

- *Exhale God, knowing that God-outside-of-you exhales you.*

- *Repeat these last two steps two more times.*

- *Recall that God is within you, breathing as you inhale.*

- *Recall that God is within you, breathing, as you exhale.*

- *Now, impossibly, paradoxically, and perfectly: God-within-you breathes in the very stuff you are made of. Inhale with this truth.*

- *Impossibly, paradoxically, perfectly: God-within-you breathes out the very stuff you are made of. Exhale this truth.*

- *Repeat any portion of this progression. Or release the words entirely.*

# Living in the Now

There is an ancient saying: "As above, so below." More recently, Richard Rohr has shared with us, "How you do anything is how you do everything." Our approach to any one thing does deeply reflect our approach to all of the things we do.

Just as it is not helpful to try to recreate yesterday's meditation, in the rest of life, living in the past, recreating the things that have already happened is not helpful either. In relationships, or seemingly mundane events, works of art, conversations, meals, jobs we sometimes have these luminous moments. Often, the fact that these were shining and exciting was rooted in the fact that they were wholly novel. To try to recapture the lived experience of their novelty, we try to recreate these experiences and find ourselves disappointed with the result.

Perhaps I have a great conversation with a loved one. I am suddenly feeling closer than I have in a long time. If I revisit the same topics of conversation later, I will likely find myself disappointed that the same fireworks do not appear. Or maybe I am scouring the refrigerators for things to put on top of my plate of nachos. The resulting configuration balances the perfect medley of sweet and savory, crunchy and gooey, pronounced and subtle. A week later I am finding myself thinking about those flavors. I remember how well the blackened onions contrasted the abundance of cilantro. When I try to recreate that precise onion-to-cilantro ratio, however, I find myself disappointed with the result. How many times have we eagerly anticipated a sequel to that powerful film or album, only to find that the followup is just a disappointing rehashing of the same things that were handled so wonderfully in the original?

I find myself returning to the topic of the destructive side of hope here. If we hope that the sequel will be as good as the original, if we hope that the new nachos will be as delicious as the old ones, and if we hope that today's meditation session will be as transformative as the last one was, we set ourselves up for failure. But we can slowly learn to accept that every moment is new and different from the prior moment. Every breath lays no claim on what the next breath will have to offer.

When we navigate our way through the hurt and reach a point of acceptance about what has happened with our old community, the temptation will be to try to recreate that same old experience we had last time. This is safe and comfortable. We have learned those lessons well. That's why there won't be much value in reliving that same scenario all over again, even if we manage to find some sort of new gloss or spin to put on the arrangement.

Discovering the essence breeds a new and different sort of humility. This humility, combined with my embrace of the world and my rejection of the past community's political agenda, all come together to make me a much more effective ally to those who are being oppressed. I find myself more interested in taking action, more aware of my internalized racism, sexism, heteronormative assumptions, and colonizer's mindset.

But humility is still important here, as I realize that my tendency to want to fix every issue and solve every problem is toxic to myself and others. I am learning that I need to close my mouth and listen more. My place is not at the front of a crowd, solving things for someone else. I need to be in the crowd, supporting those who are oppressed in solving these struggles for themselves. To deny them this role is to deny a fundamental step in their healing.

The next steps continue to be new and unknown. They are places where we are likely to make mistakes. These mistakes are a sign that we are stretching and growing. The act of discovering the essence is an ongoing process. It's understandable that a person would want to take a break from this difficult process. But it is such an important thing to return to.

## CHAPTER FIFTEEN

🌿🌿🌿🌿🌿🌿🌿🌿🌿🌿🌿🌿🌿🌿🌿🌿

# Do I Have to Incorporate the Things I Learned in the Past?

The hero's journey ends with a return to the ordinary world. Sometimes this is an ascent, a climb back from the underworld. Sometimes, this happens only after dismemberment and death and a resurrection. Sometimes, the death seemed that it would come at the hands of the great villain, but instead, there is a unification, a coming together of hero and villain.

The outside setting was never the important part. The physical distance traveled was never the best way to measure the journey. The ordinary world is recognized for what it has always been: extraordinary.

This does not mean you should return to your spiritual community. But you will see the gifts and wisdom won on this journey with new eyes. The old home will seem in some ways new. The new home will seem in some ways old. Indeed, most of us do not return physically to the place where we came from. We do not go back to that church or temple, that group or school. What does happen is this: we learn that the things we never thought were going to be gifts actually are gifts. That does not mean that everything is a gift. It does not make mistreatment okay. It simply means that when we return to the (extra) ordinary world, we have a new use for things we thought were worthless.

Our learning progresses, of course, in spirals. There will be many departures. Many journeys. Many homecomings. Strangely, eventually, you may come back to be very much the same beginner you were some time ago.

Taking such a broad, theoretical view may not be helpful, though. These mysteries and our attempts at unraveling them may not help much where you are now. So let's make this a little bit more specific and concrete.

Let's end where we began. You are going to be okay. I hope that if that was hard to hear and believe back in chapter 1, it is a little bit less so now. There likely many things that happened in the spiritual community you are leaving that were not okay. They were not okay because they hurt you, and more important, they are not okay because they were simply wrong. Unhealthy spiritual communities find these ways of intertwining themselves with our broken places. Whether intentionally or not, they exploit our human frailties and keep us subjugated and in the dark.

The irony is that the essence of a healthy spirituality is freedom in all things. Anything that shackles you is a manmade afterthought. It is far from essential. The nature of the essence is liberation. Sometimes, our own self-love and courage conspire with the fundamental nature of liberating spirituality and overpower the human trappings.

This is not easy work.

And in the process, there will be things that your once-community thinks about you. These things that they project on you are ultimately about their own fears and insecurities. Similarly, there will likely be things that seem like they are about the community that you are leaving. These things that you are feeling may well also be projections.

One of the main tasks of this journey is sorting through the feelings and uncovering the difference between projections and realities. There will be things that are easy to work through and things that are more difficult. There will be many things that are a mystery. It won't always be clear whether they are reality, projection, (or most likely) both. This is why we are called to humility and nondualistic thinking.

I am grateful for the possibility of building a spiritual practice. This will fill some of the void in the space that membership in the community used to fill. This will build tolerance for the hurt and the ambiguity of it all. This will provide a doorway through which the world that was once denied can now be embraced.

It is quite likely the hurts and the blessings of the place you came from run deeper than you can see right now. There is no need to rush to reclaim these. But left to our own devices, most of us will let them sit forever. There never seems to be a right time to begin this difficult work. It is not the case that you owe anyone else your forgiveness for whatever wrongs might have transpired. But when you are ready, offering that forgiveness will be in your best interest.

Similarly, it is not the case that you are a bad, ungrateful person if you are not able to find gratitude for the gifts that you received in the place where you were. However, when you are ready, it will be good for you to find gratitude for the gifts. It wasn't all a gift. There are elements you don't need to be thankful for. But the gifts—such as they were—come in two different forms: First, those that could be unwrapped with minimal assembly required; these are gifts that were to be used as they were intended. Second, is a variety of gift that must be repurposed. For example, if your old community force a confrontation, that challenge may ultimately be a gift, though it was not intended to be one.

I got to this place by going through all the feelings I needed to. At this time, it seems like I have worked my way through most of these things. But sometimes I am surprised and find a little reservoir of resentment that is mine to go through. There are lots of people who would have me bypass all my feelings. They would want me to walk around the scary kingdoms where these feelings dwell. Because those kingdoms were scary, they felt dangerous. But the real danger was in not walking through them.

There would be no shame if I was still in those places. No one had the right to expect me to go more quickly than I did. In truth, no one even knows how long we dwell in these liminal spaces. No one knows how long we mourn;, no one knows how long we carry anger.

This does create a real danger. There is always the danger of dwelling for longer than we needed to. There is the danger of milking these feelings and experiencing unpleasantness in ways that are not necessary.

But love is the only way we earn the right to understand someone else's suffering. Claiming we love the person is not nearly enough. If the other person does not truly love us, they do not have the authority to speak into our experiences. These lovers of our soul, they are the only people who have any right to speak to us about the possibility that we might be dwelling longer than we need to in these dark places.

And with the possibility of love, our journey comes to the essence. It may not be the journey we would have chosen for ourselves. That's all irrelevant. Our journey was our journey. In the traveling, we found the things we needed were within us. In the arrival, we find that it was never about the destination. We found that there were things we no longer needed, and we discarded them as we went. We learned some things were quite nonnegotiable, and sometimes we were surprised by what they were. This knowledge sometimes builds us up and fills us with joy. It sometimes weighs us down and fills us with sadness. This is what it is.

It was not our first journey. It won't be our last. But we are better for it, stronger and wiser. It is better than we thought it would be. And worse. Our expectations so rarely match the reality. Why should we be surprised here?

It is right and fitting that we conclude this book with a practice, and that this practice in many ways harkens back to the simplicity of our very first one. There is much value in simplicity and in complexity. I hope that you will continue to practice the more complex exercises throughout this book, but sometimes, the simplest is the best. So for today, why not return to this simple practice?

## Practice 31
## Our Final Practice

- *Sit.*
- *Breathe.*

# Dante's Road

## The Journey Home for the Modern Soul

*Nautilus Book Awards Gold Medal Winner*

This spiritual guidebook follows in the footsteps of Dante on his journey through the *Divine Comedy*. A fresh, modern take on this path, the book invites us to explore these questions: what is my hell and how do I move through it? What is my purgatory and what lesson do I need to take away? What is my paradise; how do I get there and how do I stay there? With wisdom distilled from the great myths, scriptures, and the world's mystics, this book is an invitation to ever-greater awakening and wholeness.

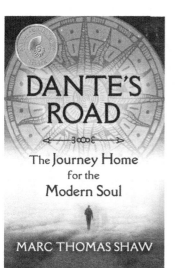

**Paperback Price: $19.95**

**Kindle Price: $5.99**

# Become Fire!

## Guideposts for
## Interspiritual Pilgrims

Bruce Epperly invites you to join him on a holy adventure in spiritual growth, inspired by the evolving wisdom of Christianity and the world's great spiritual traditions, innovative global spiritual practices, and emerging visions of reality. By embracing the diverse insights of spiritual wisdom givers, physicists, cosmologists, healing practitioners, and Earth keepers, we can meet the Earth's current challenges with love, joy, and a united strength.

**Paperback Price: $24.95**

**Kindle Price: $5.99**

# Sitting with God

## A Journey to Your True Self
## Through Centering Prayer

"This work offers a friendly and accessible approach to centering prayer that will be of great benefit to those new to the practice. Rich has a lovely way of inviting the reader in through honest reflections on his own experience, both struggles and graces. These stories offer comfort and gentle encouragement on the way."

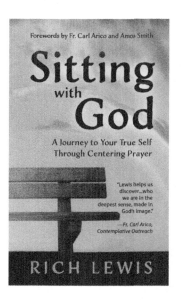

— Christine Valters Paintner, author of *The Soul of a Pilgrim*

**Paperback Price: $19.99**

**Kindle Price: $4.99**

# Hope in an Age of Fear

## Wisdom from the Book of Revelation

The Book of Revelation has been misunderstood as a book of future predictions and escape from the world—but it is actually a survival and transformation guide, written for people whose lives were threatened by the first-century system of domination. Kenneth McIntosh goes through the entire book, chapter by chapter, revealing Revelation's abundance of wisdom we can apply to the challenges we face in today's world.

**Paperback Price: $19.99**

**Kindle Price: $4.99**

# Water from an Ancient Well

## Celtic Spirituality for Modern Life

Using story, scripture, reflection, and prayer, this book offers readers a taste of the living water that refreshed the ancient Celts. The author invites readers to imitate the Celtic saints who were aware of God as a living presence in everybody and everything. This ancient perspective gives radical new alternatives to modern faith practices, ones that

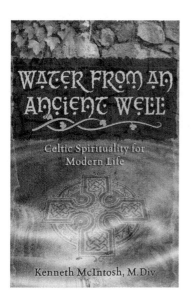

are both challenging and constructively positive. This is a Christianity big enough to embrace the entire world.

**Paperback Price: $19.99**

**Kindle Price: $5.99**

www.AnamcharaBooks.com

Printed in Great Britain
by Amazon

18894005R10202